LOST STAR

LOST STAR

THE SEARCH FOR AMELIA EARHART

RANDALL BRINK

W·W· NORTON & COMPANY

NEW YORK   LONDON

Copyright © 1993 by Randall Brink

All rights reserved

Printed in the United States of America

First published as a Norton paperback 1995

The text of this book is composed in
11.5/13.5 Goudy Old Style 291 Monotype
with the display set in
Poster Bodoni and Goudy Old Style 291 Monotype.
Composition and manufacturing by
the Haddon Craftsmen, Inc.
Book design by Margaret M. Wagner

Library of Congress Cataloging-in-Publication Data
Brink, Randall.
Lost star : the search for Amelia Earhart / by Randall Brink.
p. cm.
Includes bibliographical references and index.
1. Earhart, Amelia, 1897–1937. 2. Air pilots—United
States—Biography. 3. Government information—United
States. 4. Search and rescue operations. I. Title.
TL540.E3B72 1993
629.13'092—dc20
[B]   92-42486

ISBN 0-393-31311-5

W. W. Norton & Company, Inc.
500 Fifth Avenue, New York, N.Y. 10110
W. W. Norton & Company Ltd.
10 Coptic Street, London WC1A 1PU

3 4 5 6 7 8 9 0

Contents

Illustrations follow pages 96 and 160

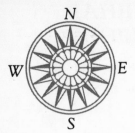

PACIFIC

MARIANA ISLANDS
  Saipan
  Guam

TRUK
ISLANDS

CAROLINE   ISLANDS

945 statute miles

NEW GUINEA
Lae

CORAL SEA

AUSTRALIA

AMELIA EARHART'S
FINAL FLIGHT

──────── The publicly announced route

▬ ▬ ▬ ▬ The actual route

O C E A N

M A R S H A L L   I S L A N D S

Maloelap Atoll
Taroa I

Jaluit   Mili Atoll

2660 statute miles

GILBERT ISLANDS   Howland I

2556 statute miles   PHOENIX
                                      ISLANDS

SOLOMON
ISLANDS   ELLICE ISLANDS

Guadalcanal
                                              SAMOA
                                              ISLANDS

                    FIJI ISLANDS

CHAZAUD

To Shelley

Acknowledgments

This book is the product of more than a decade of research, interviews, and discussions with hundreds of people, many of whom are mentioned in the pages of the book, and an equal or greater number who are not. To acknowledge them and their contributions would take most of the pages allotted for this book. I have attempted to mention their names wherever appropriate in the text, and no one has been intentionally omitted.

My editor at W. W. Norton, Mary Cunnane, is not only to be thanked, but also given a special endurance medal for perseverance and valor uncommon in publishing today. Mr. Charles Flowers's assistance with the manuscript during editing and completion is gratefully acknowledged.

I particularly wish to thank the many people who pointed the way to the information gathered for this book and whose encouragement at various critical intervals enabled its completion. Mr. Charles Schrader of the Disney Company, who started it all; the late Walter B. McMenamy who first related the truth of what happened in the planning stages of the Amelia Earhart world flight, and his friend and colleague, Karl E. Pierson, who was there at the time and corroborated McMenamy's experiences and recollections.

Lloyd Royer, friend of Amelia Earhart, and later a Lockheed employee, provided much valuable insight into the workings of the Lockheed Aircraft Company prior to and at the time of Amelia's disappearance. The late Margo DeCarrie, Amelia's aide and companion during the preparations for the world flight, provided much valuable information about what happened in the days and weeks leading up to Amelia's departure on her around-the-world flight.

Special thanks are extended to the many archivists, curators, and librarians who assisted with finding and obtaining documents, photographs, and other historical data, and grappling with the intricacies of the Freedom of Information Act in its early manifestations, including John F. Taylor, Katherine Nicastro, and Ed Marks, of the National Archives and Records Service; Charles Shaughnessy of the Navy and Old Army Branch of the National Archives; George Henriksen, recently retired as Director of the U.S. Navy Security Group Command Headquarters in Washington, D.C.; Raymond Teichman, Supervisory Archivist of the Franklin D. Roosevelt Library, Hyde Park, N.Y.; Gene M. Gressley, Director of the Western History Research Center of the University of Wyoming at Laramie, and custodian of the private papers collections of George Palmer Putnam, Eugene L. Vidal, and Captain Laurance F. Safford, USN, all of which were important to this book.

The late U.S. Ambassador to Japan, Edwin O. Reischauer is acknowledged for his graciousness in recounting key episodes of the period of the Amelia Earhart mystery, including the Japanese military and intelligence status during the 1937–41 period, as well as the mysterious "Tokyo Rose" radio broadcasts, and the 1949 Tokyo Rose/Iva Toguri D'Aquina trial.

Thanks also to Mrs. Katherine (Vidal) Smith for her vivid recollection of remarks made to her concerning the circumstances surrounding the disappearance of Amelia Earhart and Fred Noonan, by her former husband, Eugene Vidal.

My personal and professional gratitude is extended to Major Joseph Gervais, USAF (ret.), along with his wife, Thelma, for years of encouragement and hospitality at their Las Vegas residence during the course of the research and writing, as well as for providing significant evidence and information without which this book would not have been possible.

Randall Brink
Twin Lakes, Idaho
October 25, 1993

"Never let your left hand know what your right is doing," Franklin Roosevelt once advised Henry Morgenthau, Jr.

"Which hand am I?" Morgenthau asked.

"My right hand," FDR answered, "but I keep my left hand under the table."

Introduction

The question is fair: why, more than five decades after Amelia Earhart and her navigator, Fred Noonan, vanished in the Pacific, should yet another answer to the mystery be proposed in print?

As it happens, there are several very good reasons, some of them startling and even unsettling, particularly to those of us who like to believe that, in the long run, the U.S. government eventually comes clean with the American people.

For one thing, despite a continuing flood over the years of speculative articles and books, despite numerous military, government, and amateur investigations, not one shred of evidence has ever been brought forward to support the generally accepted, conventional, "official" version: i.e., that Earhart ditched her plane in the ocean and died there on July 2, 1937.

The accepted version is no more likely to be true than other, equally plausible solutions that require that Earhart and Noonan disappear without a trace. In the absence of proof, for example, it is just as possible that they landed on one of the hundreds of uncharted small islands in the wide bowl of the Pacific and perished of starvation and exposure . . . or that they landed on an island occupied by the Japanese and were summarily executed as spies. The accepted version has the virtue of simplicity and finality; that is the source of its appeal. The other plausible versions that have been proposed by legions of investigators, researchers, and writers have the appeal of the exotic, the unsanctioned; but, though the speculations may have ranged from the reasonable to the lunatic, they all share an essential characteristic with the accepted version: lack of proof.

In short, one sufficient reason to explore the disappearance of Amelia Earhart yet again is that it has never been solved.

But this book, the culmination of ten years' worth of research, travel, adventure, and hassles with government bureaucrats, was inspired by two developments that have made it possible to unlock secrets kept from public view for half a century.

By 1980, the Freedom of Information Act was enacted. For the first time, as will become evident, certain critically revealing documents about the Earhart case could be prized from official government files. (To be sure, the process is cumbersome and time-consuming, and this author still has several cases pending for the release of information retained by recalcitrant officials.) These new items of hard evidence convincingly support my solution to the Earhart story, even in aspects that on their surface would seem incredible and bizarre.

Also in 1980, a serendipitous encounter, perhaps appropriately combining elements of Hollywood with aviation, unveiled a central part of the Earhart mystery. At the time, I was managing editor of *Air Progress*, a civil-aviation magazine based in Los Angeles, after working as captain on a commercial airline. Like almost everyone involved in aviation, I had been intrigued by the historic riddle but considered it solved, or unsolvable, an anomaly of history, like Hitler's decision not to press on to Moscow, or the disappearance of the Lost Tribe of Roanoke. I certainly had no interest in setting out to investigate the mystery myself. But one morning, out of the blue, I received a call from a man named Charles Schrader at Walt Disney Studios concerning an intriguing story. Someone claiming to have secret information about Amelia Earhart's last flight thought his story would make a good film. To Schrader, it sounded more like an investigative story; in any case, it wasn't Disney material.

I considered the tip with considerable skepticism. How likely could it be that a reliable, informed source had kept quiet all these years? Or would, to put it baldly, still have a memory that could be trusted? In the event, I would discover that Walter B. McMenamy, alert and highly intelligent at eighty-five years of age despite failing health, did indeed have a credible story to tell. As will become clear in my account, he provided the impetus that set me down the path of a decade-long search for the truth.

I would discover evidence that our government lied about, and continues to conceal, the truth in the Amelia Earhart affair. I would discover pieces to the puzzle in the South Pacific, on remote and forgotten particles of land where she touched down that morning in July 1937 and afterward. But most of the story would have to be ferreted out of long-secret storage, one piece at a time: in the U.S. Army classified counterintelligence files, in a secret FBI case report, from within a mass of yellowing radio reports, and from veritable mounds of Naval Intelligence files, classified for four decades and housed in an obscure military repository in an unnamed Midwestern town. These were the American sources; there would also be a strange clue from the imperial government of Japan.

Even so, until still other hidden details are brought to
light, as I believe they eventually will be, the story I have
uncovered does not go beyond the end of 1937. From
then until 1945, Amelia's trail grows progressively colder,
as accurate information about her fate becomes progressively more scarce. Finally, from about September 1945,
the truth about her ultimate fate becomes shrouded in
rumor, speculation, and sketchy bits of evidence that are
as tantalizing as they are contradictory. Did she die in an
aircraft accident in China in 1945? Did she return secretly
to the U.S., assume a new identity, and live a comfortable,
upper-middle-class life until her death from natural causes
in 1983?

I leave the answers to those and similar speculations to
future investigators. In this book, I deal only with the
truth about Amelia Earhart's last flight, a truth withheld
by our government because of a tenuous peace with Japan
in the Pacific and concerns for the national security at
home. Incredibly, the cover-up continues, even though
the mystery, according to the Associated Press, can be
considered among the top ten news stories of the century.
At the time, the Amelia Earhart affair frequently occupied
the front pages of newspapers around the world for at
least two months. For sixteen days, a large task force involving ships from the U.S. Navy's Pacific Fleet and the
navies of two other nations mounted an extensive air, sea,
and land search. They would comb the vast surface of the
ocean and the widely scattered lagoons and atolls of the
Central Pacific region, including the Line Islands, Phoenix
Islands, and Gilbert Islands: a huge total area of more than
a quarter of a million square miles.

For public consumption, the U.S. Navy concluded that
the plucky, charismatic aviator and her skilled navigator
were "lost at sea." The official finding was believed by
most people; that was the way of things in those days.

There were a few skeptics, of course, but, then, there are people today who believe that all of the moon landings were staged in the Arizona desert. The number of people who were actually involved in the Earhart episode, who possessed firsthand knowledge of the facts, was very small.

Small, but important and powerful: those who knew the truth, and held it close, knew that Earhart and Noonan had survived. They believed it was their duty to hide the truth, and so they did.

How and why this was done, the details of the circumstances that led to Earhart's disappearance and what happened to her afterward, and how I finally obtained this information, are the subject of this book.

Author's Note

To understand how a government cover-up could succeed in 1937, it is only necessary to recall how much the world has changed. The Pacific was farther away, in effect, because communications were primitive. Even today, much of the area is uncharted.

In addition, the public was distracted throughout the late 1930s by other major stories: the aftermath of the Lindbergh kidnapping, Guernica and the Spanish Civil War, the unprovoked Japanese attack on the U.S. gunboat *Panay* in China's Yangtze River, Italy's alliance with Hitler's Germany, and the growing fears that a militarily unprepared America was in grave danger from German and Japanese expansionism.

Finally, decades before Watergate, the relationship between press and government was hardly adversarial, nor were officials automatically suspected of engaging in "disinformation." Investigative information as we know it today did not exist. (As a practical matter, furthermore, the news media simply did not have the capacity to cover Earhart's flight independently.

U.S. government personnel could secretly control the flight operation and the release of any and all information about it.) To take only one example of journalists' trust of government, in the immediate aftermath of Earhart's disappearance, the pages of the nation's press were duly filled with vilifications of stunt flying, including criticism of the public expenditure naturally and inevitably necessitated by the "sport." In other words, her last flight was helpfully portrayed as one woman's idiosyncratic adventure, just as Roosevelt wanted it to be played.

Today the cover-up continues. During the ten years I researched this account, the government consistently refused to release fifty-year-old documents pertinent to this investigation.

Some of the bureaucratic obstacles may have less to do with an institution's desire to conceal information than with the enormous number of classified documents maintained by the government and the lack of efficient methods of processing them for research use. In theory, a document or file that is classified—i.e., withheld from the public in the interest of national security—stays in the system until it is reviewed for declassification or destroyed. In practice, as the millions upon millions of pieces of paper and rolls of microfilm in storage attest, classified material is seldom destroyed.

To compound the problem, the existing system for routine declassification is archaic, technically deficient, fiscally handicapped, and grossly understaffed. Nor does anyone really know just how many tons of material are stored in the dozens of warehouses all across the country, much less what is in them. Government archivists cannot locate even the material known to exist, because there is no standardized system for taking inventory or cataloguing. On shelves in the dark, labyrinthine corridors of the National Archives building in Washington, D.C., as in other repositories, documents are kept in boxes or in ancient cloth-bound volumes, a nearly untappable embarrassment of riches. Or consider the more than fourteen thousand rolls of microfilm stored in cool, dry vaults in the several warehouses of the navy's installation at Crane, Indiana. Each roll holds approximately 350 feet of 16mm microfilm, with something like one hundred documents per foot. Most of these approximately five hundred million documents date from World War II and before. Microfilm, of the type and size used then is now becoming obsolete, and procuring the equipment for viewing and reproducing it is expensive and difficult. Navy officials estimate that they will complete their FOIA review at Crane sometime after the year 2021.

Another problem specific to this book is that there is not, as one might assume in such a highly publicized and politically sensitive case, any such thing as an "Amelia Earhart file." The crucial elements of my discovery were scattered throughout the vast jungle of classified and declassified material. I was fortunate enough to find many clues, but more exist. The State Department, for example, released vital pieces of evidence as recently as July 2, 1987—ironically, the fiftieth anniversary of Earhart's disappearance. (See telegram, illus. 15.)

Finally, the FOIA itself is not obstacle-free. In fact, it is a perfect Catch-22. Contrary to popular belief, the act does not require a government agency to review all of its classified material for declassification. Nor is the researcher allowed to sift through the files in search of something of interest. He or she must request a specific document, photograph, or other item. That is the catch: in order to request a document, you must know what it specifically contains.

Nonetheless, the FOIA is a blessing; without it, the mystery of Amelia Earhart's last flight would most certainly never have been solved. For example, the photograph reproduced as illus. 11—not released from the Defense Intelligence Section in Suitland, Maryland, despite repeated requests, until I accidentally discovered its existence and probable subject—was critically important.

In the long run, I suspect, the public will have access to all of the U.S. government files relating to the mystery. Perhaps we may someday learn what information, if any, is held in the Japanese archives, as yet completely untouched. For the present, however, I can say with assurance that the new information I've found solves the essential riddle: what happened in the last hours of the famous flight, and did Amelia Earhart survive?

The world is a better place to live in because it contains human beings who will give up ease and security and stake their own lives in order to do what they themselves think worth doing . . . who are brave without cruelty to others and impassioned with an idea that dignifies all who contemplate it. . . .

The best things of mankind are as useless as Amelia Earhart's adventure. . . . In such persons mankind overcomes the inertia which would keep it earthbound forever in its habitual ways. They have found in them the free and useless energy with which alone men surpass themselves.

Such energy cannot be planned and managed. It is wild and free. But all the heroes, the saints and the seers, the explorers and the creators, partake of it. They do not know what they discover. They do not know where their impulse is taking them.

They have been possessed for a time with an extraordinary passion which is unintelligible in ordinary human terms.

They do the useless, brave, noble, the divinely foolish and the very wisest things that are done by man. And what they prove to themselves and to others is that man is no mere automaton in his routine, no mere cog in the collective machine, but that in the dust of which he is made there is also fire, lighted now and then by great winds from the sky.

—Walter Lippmann, *New York Times*

LOST STAR

CHAPTER ONE

Lae

LAE, NEW GUINEA, July 2—Amelia Earhart departed
for Howland Island at 10 o'clock today beginning a
2,556-mile flight across the Pacific along a route
never traveled before by an airplane. Miss Earhart's
Wasp-motored Lockheed Electra plane made a
difficult take-off with ease, but it was only fifty
yards from the end of the runway when it rose into
the air.[1]

ABOARD CUTTER *ITASCA* off Howland Island, July 2
(AP)—United States sailors and Coastguardsmen
set watch tonight along one of the loneliest
stretches of the earth's surface to guide Amelia Earhart on the longest, most hazardous flight of her career. The *Itasca* and the cutter *Ontario* awaited
word of her take-off from Lae for Howland Island,
an almost microscopic bit of land representing
America's frontier in the South Pacific.

From the very beginning, the public per-
ception and the hidden truth about Amelia
Earhart's last flight were entirely different.
Let us begin with the "cover story," perhaps only vaguely remembered or even en-

tirely forgotten now, but intensely exciting to people living in the quieter world between the wars.

When thirty-nine-year-old Earhart took off from Lae
on July 2, 1937, in her twin-engine Lockheed Electra, she
was supposedly on one of the last legs of an ambitious and
risky attempt to make a new aviation record: the first
round-the-world flight at the equator. The announced
plan called for her to fly 2,556 miles across the Pacific to a
tiny speck of land, Howland Island, in the isolated Line
Islands, some eighteen hundred miles west of Hawaii.
During the previous month, she had piloted the Electra
more than twenty-five thousand miles, about twenty-two
thousand miles (or 80 percent of the total distance around
the world) on this record attempt. Perhaps surprisingly, in
light of her legendary status as the first and most daring of
women aviators, she intended this venture to be her last
flight. Her many headline-catching feats had been grueling
and frightening, particularly when she had to cross wide
stretches of ocean for hours at a time. Besides, she felt that
she had already achieved her main goal, to prove that
women could do anything men could do.

Thus far, on this flight alone, she had reported in from
some of the most remote and exotic spots on the globe,
using the day's technology to swoop down on places that
had inspired the romantic travel tales of nineteenth-cen-
tury male adventurers: Paramaribo in Dutch Guiana; Fortaleza, Brazil; Dakar, Senegal; El Fasher, in what was then
known as French Equatorial Africa; Khartoum, in the
Anglo-Egyptian Sudan; Karachi, Eritrea, beside the Red
Sea; Calcutta, East India, on the banks of the Ganges;
Bandoeng, Java, and many more.[2]

One of the most famous women in the world, Earhart
had been making history as well as headlines for a decade
and a half. It began in 1922, when she set an altitude record for women by climbing her tiny Kinner Sport bi-

plane above fourteen thousand feet.[3] In 1928, she became
the first woman to cross the Atlantic by air, although she
was not at the controls of the airplane.[4] Between 1928 and
1935, Earhart set three transcontinental air records:
becoming the first woman to fly a solo round-trip across
the U.S. and establishing two nonstop speed records. On
April 8, 1931, she twice broke the altitude record for the
autogiro, a peculiar contraption that was a hybrid of airplane and helicopter. First she flew up to a record fifteen
thousand feet, then broke her own record later in the
same day by climbing above eighteen thousand feet. She
became the first woman to fly the Atlantic alone in 1932.
In 1935, she became the first person to fly the Pacific
Ocean from Honolulu to California, to solo from Los
Angeles to Mexico City, and to solo from Mexico to Newark, New Jersey.[5]

Inevitably, Amelia Earhart, America's "First Lady of
the Air," became an icon of 1930s style and daring. Tall,
slimly attractive, usually shown flashing a bright but
somehow reserved smile, she appeared frequently on the
covers of women's magazines, in newspaper features, and
in the popular Pathé and Movietone newsreels, just as
likely to be behind the wheel of her racy Cord convertible
as at the controls of an airplane. Her outdoorsy, athletic
appearance and startling resemblance to her contempo-
rary Charles Lindbergh had earned her the nickname
"Lady Lindy," which she detested. Even so, she underscored the likeness by habitually wearing trousers and a
man's shirt under a scuffed leather jacket, and she kept her
hair short and boyishly tousled. But she could also model
the latest women's fashions, or set the styles, in glamorous
studio photographs. Millions of women imitated the several images of Amelia Earhart.

But, like Lindbergh, she had gained fame because—as
would not become evident until much later—the late

1930s were when the last great feats of private achievement in aviation took place. The public sector (i.e., the military) was not yet directly involved, because of economic and political constraints. The so-called Golden Age of Aviation coincided with the depths of the Great Depression. Little money was available for any military purpose, including the development and deployment of military aviation. In addition, the watchword of the day was "isolationism." Despite disquieting warnings from abroad that foreign military might was on the rampage, there was no political support for building up the military, even in such relatively benign areas as research and development of technology. Aviation therefore, both as aviation and as science, was still the domain of private enterprise.

And challenges were met by uniquely gifted, determined individuals, unfettered by bureaucracy or virtually any other restrictions. By 1937, Earhart had flown many different airplanes, ranging from the Kinner Sport biplane to the large single-engine Lockheed Vega monoplanes in which she set many of her records. In effect, her flying skills and her airplanes developed in tandem. The larger, more advanced Lockheed Electra of her round-the-world attempt in 1937, her last flight,[6] was indeed the most technologically sophisticated aircraft of the day, "state-of-the-art" for the late 1930s.

She once described her work space in that particular craft with her characteristic brisk wryness:

> The dimensions of my cubbyhole are four feet eight inches high, four feet six inches fore and aft. . . . Realize, too, that nearly every inch of floor, wall, and ceiling is covered with equipment. There are considerably more than a hundred gadgets in a modern cockpit that the pilot must periodically look at or twiddle.[7]

In the cockpit of the polished silver Electra (named, like all Lockheeds, for a celestial constellation), the instrument panel held an array of fifty-odd flight and air-navigation instruments. These included a simple turn-and-bank "inclinometer," which merely indicated whether or not the plane was upright or to what degree it might be turning around its three axes: that is, yawing, slipping, or sliding off a true track in the air. There were also a Kollsman sensitive altimeter, which was basically nothing more than a diaphragm-type aneroid barometer designed to show the aircraft's altitude above sea level; an airspeed-indicator reading in miles per hour (unlike today's gauges, which use knots, the international metric standard); and a primitive gyroscopic artificial-horizon instrument that provided a pictorial representation of the attitude of the aircraft in relation to the natural horizon. By the morning of her takeoff from Lae, Earhart had worked in this airborne "office" for more than 150 hours, encountering virtually all types of weather. In addition, a primitive autopilot, the Sperry Gyro-Pilot, was capable of keeping the plane's wings level but could not, like today's systems, hold an altitude, steer a course, or navigate.

In front of the pilot's leather seat were two steering wheels similar to those in automobiles, one directly in front, the other in front of the copilot's seat, on the right of the cabin (unused on this trip). Between the two seats, on a pedestal, were levers to control the throttles, engine-fuel mixture, and carburetor air-intake heat. The latter was essential to prevent ice from choking off the flow of fuel in the much colder temperature of high altitude. On a panel below this pedestal were instruments for monitoring, very precisely, the fuel flow to the two powerful Pratt & Whitney Wasp radial engines. To allow the pilot to reduce, or "lean," the fuel-to-air mixture, thus reducing fuel consumption to the absolute minimum, there were a twin-banked pair of gauges called "fuel analyzers" and "fuel-flow meters."

Finally, as would become an essential factor in the confusion surrounding Earhart's final flight, there were some radios, but they were very rudimentary.

A Bendix communications radio was capable of transmitting and receiving both voice and Morse code. Then there was an experimental, secret ADF (automatic direction-finder), intended to "home" or point directly toward almost any signal transmitted in the low-frequency range, such as other voice and code transmissions, air- or surface-borne navigation-broadcast stations, and commercial-broadcast stations.[8] Although unproved as yet, this was a remarkable example of radio wizardry for its time; even U.S. military aircraft did not carry it. But, to put things in proper perspective, any airplane so equipped today would scarcely be able to leave the airport traffic pattern, much less make a globe-girdling record flight.

Around the cockpit at various places, Earhart had put such basic items as maps, a notebook, pencils, and a thermos bottle. On the cabin ceiling, to her right, was attached a bamboo fishing rod, rigged so that she and her navigator, Fred Noonan, could pass messages back and forth, since talking to each other was impossible during flight because of the pounding noise of the engines. Directly behind the pilot's seat, huge gasoline tanks nearly filled the Electra's cabin interior. The tanks held enough fuel to fly three thousand miles, a "reserve" in excess of that actually required to fly the 2,556 miles from Lae to Howland. Just behind, and barely visible in the tiny rear compartment about nine feet behind Earhart, was Noonan, who was surrounded in his cramped space by an arrangement of air-navigation maps and oceanographic charts. His celestial-navigation sighting instruments, a "sextant" and a "bubble octant," would be used to establish the position of the plane in relation to the stars during the long overwater flight.

The forty-four-year-old Noonan, a tall, slim Irishman, had led quite an adventurous life himself, and the question of his real character may have a bearing on the Earhart mystery. At fifteen, he had run off to sea on one of the last of the legendary square-riggers. In World War I, he first served aboard a munitions carrier in the Atlantic, then joined the Royal Navy, only to have three ships torpedoed out from under him. In twenty-two years at sea, he made the treacherous Cape Horn passage seven times and was credited with saving at least a dozen lives. He learned to fly in the 1920s, became a flying instructor, and eventually specialized in applying the techniques of ocean navigation to air navigation.

In 1930, he joined Pan American Airways as a flying-boat pilot, rose to senior navigator, then became the firm's general inspector of airports. By 1935, he was in charge of planning all Pan Am routes across the Pacific and in fact served as navigator that year on the famous China Clipper flight that ushered in the age of commercial air transportation over that vast sea. On November 22, under Captain Edward Musick, the passenger plane left San Francisco for Hong Kong, stopping along the way at Hawaii, Guam, Midway, Wake, and the Philippines.

Suddenly, however, the extremely competent Noonan and his employer parted company. According to many accounts, the navigator, who could easily put away a quart of whiskey a day, lost one too many rounds to the bottle and was fired. If that was the case, his trip with Earhart could be seen as a chance to redeem himself in a notoriously unforgiving profession and make a kind of comeback. According to other versions of the story, however, Noonan quit his job with Pan Am on his own initiative, because he was saddled with administrative duties that prevented him from realizing his true ambition, to become a Clipper pilot.[9] Whatever the truth, the parting may well have been amicable, as will become clear later. In collusion with his former employer and the U.S. government, Noonan may have been using his rather rakish image as boozer and general all-around ne'er-do-well to cover his actual role as intelligence agent on Earhart's flight.[10]

On the other hand, hearsay claims that he went on a two-day binge as soon as they landed in Lae, winding up staying out most of the night before the July 2 takeoff with his host and new drinking buddy, Jim Collopy, the New Guinea district superintendent of aviation. Supposedly, Earhart had disapproved and tried to bring an end to the debauch, without success. According to Harry Balfour, a radio operator working for Air New Guinea on the island, Noonan and his cohort dragged themselves into their hotel at about 7:30 a.m., not long before Earhart knocked on her navigator's door to wake him for the next leg of their flight.[11]

Was Noonan so seriously impaired that he was a danger to their survival? It is difficult to believe that Earhart, who knew him well, would misjudge his capacity to rouse himself and work capably. It is difficult, too, to know what credence to give to stories about marathon drinking bouts, particularly in the tropics. Tall tales abound, and so do long naps after a few rounds of punch. Apparently, Collopy told Earhart that Noonan was dressing, and promised to drive him over to the airport soon. Then he woke up the red-eyed navigator, who would be sitting in his cockpit position in less than two hours, directing his pilot over a route no one had ever before flown.

Imprudent as his behavior might seem, it does not hurt to remember that Noonan and his ilk were indeed adventurers, but survivors, too. As he (and Earhart) well knew, the critical part of his task would not come until several hours later, well into the flight, when he could have caught up on his sleep and recovered from the effects of any over-indulgence. In any event, hung-over or not, Fred Noonan was a superb navigator, probably the best in the world, and certainly the one most familiar with this region of the globe. In terms of experience and natural ability, few if any other human beings were as well suited to the task of guiding the Electra safely to the tiny speck of uninhabited land called Howland Island. There, on the most minus-cule and remote landing site of the trip, the U.S. govern-ment had prepared a landing strip provisioned with fuel and oil.

And near that atoll, as a precaution, the U.S. Coast Guard cutter *Itasca* swung at anchor. Under Commander Warner K. Thompson, who will figure importantly in this story, the crew stood ready to provide a communications link for Earhart and, if necessary, to provide other assist-ance. (As we will see, this arrangement completely sup-planted a previously arranged worldwide network of civil-ian amateur radio operators, for reasons that go to the heart of the truth about the hidden purposes of the flight.)

In sum, at 9:30 a.m. that July 2, when Amelia Earhart started the engines and set the throttles at idle for a mo-ment, letting them warm up before demanding full power from them, there was as little reason to fear for the out-come of this leg of the flight as for any other, perhaps even less. The balmy skies, half filled with cumulus clouds, and calm winds marked an improvement in the weather of the previous few days. Noonan may have slept no more than two hours the night before, but that was nothing new. He had always come through for her before. Perhaps because of the extra load of fuel, though, the takeoff was not smooth. As a bystander filmed the action with a small hand-held 8mm motion-picture camera, the Electra nearly vaulted off the end of the runway before managing to struggle into the air and soar off into the rising sun of the eastern sky.

About twenty-one hours later (and still July 2 because they had crossed the international date line), according to historical tradition, pilot, navigator, and plane vanished at sea. We are to believe that, after more than twenty-two thousand miles of successful flight and navigation over some of the world's most remote and inaccessible regions, Earhart and Noonan ran out of fuel, ditched their craft in the ocean, and drowned.

This is not what happened.

Consider the hint dropped by Fleet Admiral Chester W. Nimitz, who was named commander-in-chief of the Pacific Fleet four years after Earhart apparently vanished, and later became chief of naval operations. In the 1960s, while still on active duty and unable to divulge his full knowledge, Nimitz intimated through an aide that the real story would "stagger the imagination."[12]

Consider simple logic: people and airplanes do not vanish without a trace. Yet not a sliver of airplane wreckage or debris, no scrap of metal or paper, no oil slick, no human remains, or any other tangible evidence of a ditching at sea was ever found.[13] Consider also that, at the conclusion of the most massive land-and-sea search in history, the U.S. government issued no official statement about the disappearance of Earhart and Noonan. And has not to this day.

The reason is, quite simply, that the pair survived, inadvertently touching off a complicated series of events about which the U.S. government knew a great deal more than it revealed, but which it eventually sought to cover up in order to prevent an early start to World War II in the

Pacific. Amelia Earhart was, in the end, caught up in a vortex created by the conflicting forces of her time: imperialism, isolationism, economic depression. She fell victim to a series of tragic circumstances involving her own government in high international intrigue, but she was not exactly an innocent bystander. For many months, she had known what risks lay ahead.

CHAPTER TWO

The Heroine

Not much more than a month ago, I was on the
other shore of the Pacific, looking westward. This
evening, I looked eastward over the Pacific. In those
fast-moving days which have intervened, the whole
width of the world has passed behind us—except
this broad ocean. I shall be glad when we have the
hazards of its navigation behind us.

—Amelia Earhart's last press release,
Lae, New Guinea

The specific circumstances that brought
Earhart to that last hazardous leg of her
flight, involving her in a covert government
operation that went awry, began back in
1935, as we shall see later in the book. Long
before then implacable forces had been set
in motion on the international scene that
would change the course of world history,
and of the aviation heroine's life.

But we should take a moment to look
briefly at the woman herself: the personal
adversities she faced, the forceful and determined nature of her character, her apparently contradictory political beliefs,

and her seemingly peculiar marriage to the rich publisher who managed her public career. After all, it is likely that many of today's readers will know little about Amelia Earhart, or will have been misled by the romantic and persistent blend of fantasy and fact that is the accepted image of this very complex human being.

Amelia Mary Earhart, as befits an all-American heroine, came straight from the heartland. The older of two daughters, she was born in Atchison, Kansas, on July 24, 1897, in her grandparents' house, just six years before the Wright brothers achieved the first powered human flight, at Kitty Hawk.

In her earliest years, she would enjoy a comfortably prosperous family life in Kansas City, but the strains in her parents' marriage, which became all too evident later, must have taken their toll even then. Her mother, Amy, was the daughter of a wealthy and powerful judge, Alfred Otis. Marriage to Edwin Earhart, a lawyer working at the very bottom rung of legal practice as a railroad-claims agent, brought a drop in her standard of living, even though her father had been able to give her a furnished house as a wedding present. She and her husband felt the disparity keenly. Aside from whatever insecurity or resentment Edwin might have felt about his father-in-law's wealth, the obscure young Midwestern lawyer set for himself an impossible goal: appointment to the United States Supreme Court.[1]

In reality, it was all he could do to provide the minimal income necessary to win Judge Otis's reluctant consent to his marriage to Amy. Earhart was merely an employee of the Rock Island Railroad, his days bogged down in such small matters as negotiating settlements for livestock killed on the tracks and contracting for rights-of-way. He was paid strictly on a fee basis, earning a percentage of whatever money he saved the railroad in legal settlements.

Amelia's arrival and the birth of her sister, Muriel Grace, two years later brought increasing financial burdens, of course, and Earhart's fantasies of financial and political success were apparently crushed by the realities of his life.

But Amy's proud, stubborn devotion to her husband did not waver. In fact, her obsessive concern for his success and self-esteem generally took precedence over her maternal responsibilities. Because Edwin's unpredictable income often depended upon his successfully settling claims against the railroad, she regularly left home to travel with him and offer support when he had to go out of town to negotiate a case.

Amelia, the firstborn, adapted well to these absences, which were frequently extended, and other changes in her circumstances. Not unlike many older children, she exuded a sense of independence and self-confidence, traits that were nurtured by her attentively doting maternal grandparents. The two girls spent each winter in the well-appointed Otis home in Atchison, summers back in Kansas City with their parents. This regular shuttling back and forth between extravagant circumstances and genteel poverty ended in 1908, when Amelia was eleven. That year, Edwin took a salaried position in the Rock Island Railroad's claims department in Des Moines. With his new job and a new home, the family experienced the rich promise of a fresh slate.[2]

Amy, despite her privileged and even cosseted background, adjusted contentedly to domestic routine in Iowa. She learned to cook, and she taught her daughters to sew. Ironically, her daughter Amelia, who was an enthusiastic student, would one day profit greatly from these lessons. When she became famous, her unconventional flying attire captured the fancy of women across the country. She was persuaded to help promote her flights by designing a line of casual clothing. (Thanks to her mother,

Amelia also had some experience in idiosyncratic fashion. Amy's sister, a devotee of the noted feminist Mrs. Bloomer, persuaded her to send the girls to school decked out in the infamous loose pants known as "bloomers" while they were still in elementary school.)[3]

In Des Moines, the Earharts tried for a while to keep private tutors for their daughters, who had always attended a private academy during their winter sojourns in Atchison. For financial reasons, however, Amelia and Muriel were soon enrolled in the nearest public school. But something more important occurred. For the first time, the family experienced shared contentment, a sense of togetherness. A relaxed Edwin enjoyed entertaining his daughters, and often their new playmates in the neighborhood as well, with his wonderful stories and delightfully imaginative games. He and Amelia, who both played piano by ear, spent hours together at the keyboard. Because his abilities were certainly not inconsiderable, Earhart was quickly promoted to department chief. For his company travels, which often took him as far away as California, he was assigned a private railroad car, and his wife and daughters frequently accompanied him on business trips.[4]

Unfortunately, the marriage, which had endured the constant threat of imminent impoverishment, began to founder because of a new problem. Edwin's new financial stability was provided by a job that left him bored and profoundly dissatisfied. By 1910, he had begun to drink heavily and neglect his work. The downward spiral of his depression, exacerbated by alcohol, led to episodes of emotional abuse at home and occasional outright violence.[5]

Thirteen-year-old Amelia, stung to the core by the sudden betrayal of a father who had once loved and indulged her, began to exhibit behavior that would today be recognized as typical of the oldest child of an alcoholic. Initially, she tried to rescue Edwin from himself. But in one instance, when he discovered that she had emptied his whiskey bottle down the drain in the kitchen sink, he tried to hit her.[6] As her influence over him vanished, she began to feel a sense of helplessness and unconscious guilt. Repelled as well as frightened, Amelia withdrew to the relative safety of rebellion, siding against him in an alliance with her mother and sister, Muriel. She began to adopt an attitude toward both parents, usurping their authority, that was frequently condescending if not domineering and insolent.

Of course, the family's problem was a matter to be concealed. Alcoholism, not understood as a disease in those days, carried the great threat of social stigma, particularly for the relatives of a prominent judge.[7] Amy kept the truth from her aging parents, fearful they would take drastic measures to protect her inheritance from the incompetent management of her drunken husband. She would be proved right when her father died. The widowed Mrs. Otis finally learned about Edwin's problem and immediately restructured her will so that Amy's share of the estate would be placed in trust for twenty years or until Edwin's death, whichever should occur first. This was, of course, the ultimate insult to a son-in-law who had never been fully accepted by his wife's parents.

Worse, the railroad had begun to notice his erratic and often incompetent handling of its legal affairs. When an official from the legal department in the head office popped in unannounced one day, Edwin was drunk at his desk. He was summarily fired.[8] Chastened, Amelia's father took the cure, but the humiliation of public exposure made it difficult for him to honor his vow to abstain, and he embarked on what appeared to be an endless bout of drinking.

The family separated. The unemployable Edwin was put into the care of relatives in Kansas City, while Amy and the girls went to Chicago to live with old friends of the Otis family. Enrolled in Hyde Park High School, teenaged Amelia excelled at science and math, showing an ability to solve difficult problems quickly, but exasperating her teachers by stubbornly refusing to explain her unique methods of doing so. Explanations, she thought, were unnecessary and a waste of her time; the solution to a problem was the important thing, not the means to that end. She had become adept, as well, at concealing her feelings and personal secrets.

Already strongly evident, in other words, were the independence and distaste for convention that would characterize her behavior in adulthood. To take another example, she developed a masterful command of language, as would be made impressively clear in her formal correspondence and her books and articles. But in her personal letters, and occasionally in her flight journals, she delighted in slaughtering the king's English with deliberate misspellings, send-ups of American dialects, exaggerated idioms, and idiosyncratic abbreviations. The result is a humorous and endearing quality, which she would often use in letters to her mother to soften a particularly condescending or controlling stance. This linguistic playfulness began in her teens, perhaps as a distraction from the harsh realities of her sundered family life.

So, too, did her commitment to serious scholarship and budding convictions that would today be called feminist. However spontaneous she might seem on paper, she was in fact confronting life and her future with frowning intensity, and had pinned her hopes on attending Bryn Mawr or Vassar.[9] Unfortunately, Edwin would inadvertently stand in her way.

For, soon after Amelia graduated from Hyde Park in

June 1915, her parents were reconciled and the family re-united in Kansas City, where Edwin was working as a law-yer. Tuition for Amelia's college education, as well as Muriel's, would have been handled under the terms of the Otis trust, but Earhart persuaded Amy to contest her mother's will, on the basis that it was being poorly admin-istered. In fact, the $250,000 principal sum had indeed dwindled down to $60,000. Although the suit would even-tually succeed, the legal challenge delayed Amelia's appli-cation to Vassar. She settled instead on the Ogontz School, a private women's college near Philadelphia.[10]

Actually, the maturing Amelia was happy for any es-cape from her family situation, of which she did not ap-prove. Her adolescent rebellion had evolved into indigna-tion against the injustice of the social codes her parents had allowed to dominate their lives, from the deception and secrecy to the impotent role her mother was forced to assume. Amelia wanted no part of such a scheme.

On the other hand, to judge from her letters home from Pennsylvania, she was not really disposed to self-analysis, to consideration of what she might want instead. Far from expressing her innermost thoughts, her correspondence, almost exclusively addressed to Amy, gave accounts of her social activities and involvement in student govern-ment, along with scathing indictments of the school's headmistress. Poignantly, the pages and pages of descrip-tions of other people on campus reveal little about her relationships with them, or any indication of genuine inti-macy.

Apparently popular, however, Amelia was elected to a number of campus offices and busied herself with various projects and organizations, assuming an amazing number of responsibilities. On this score, she often had to reas-sure Amy, who thought her daughter was risking ill health by taking on so much.

Perhaps the frantic activity was the predictable, if un-conscious, protective barrier against closeness. Implicit in any intimacy for her had always been the threat of pain, after her father's betrayal and the constant interruptions in her relationships with parents and grandparents. Per-haps she would never be able to commit herself to another human being with any degree of real loyalty. Rather, after failing to help her troubled father, she seemed to cast her-self in the role of rescuer in terms of large causes, once she decided they were truly worthy. People not infrequently do set out to save the world when they despair of saving themselves or those closest to them, of course. For young Amelia, the ultimate worthy cause appeared in the form of World War I.

At first, she had contributed rather casually to the war effort, while still at Ogontz, by knitting the occasional sweater and volunteering to roll bandages. But in 1917, when she spent her senior-year Christmas break in Toronto with her mother and Muriel, she became fully aware of the horrors of war. On the streets of the city, she frequently encountered hideously crippled young men who had just arrived from the front or been dismissed from the hospital. Back on campus in Pennsylvania, she could not shake the images of men who had lost their limbs or minds in the inferno of trench warfare. This was the beginning of her lifelong belief in pacifism. With Amy's permission, she abandoned her studies and re-turned to Toronto to become a volunteer nurse's aide.[11]

There she would have yet another life-changing experi-ence. With Muriel, she went to a flying exposition, and found herself watching in an ecstasy of horror as an air-plane and its pilot seemed to fall toward her out of the sky, then recovered power to glide gently to a perfect landing. Delighted by this rudimentary stunt, Amelia would never forget the "little red airplane."[12]

For nearly a year, she devoted herself tirelessly to nursing, exhibiting a selfless courage and taking on even the most menial, laborious tasks of housekeeping and sanitation. She also came up with drastically needed improvements in the hospital diet. Meanwhile, what she saw every day deeply confirmed her disgust for war. Years later, in 1935, her experiences led to the sarcastic, Swiftian proposal in *The Home Magazine* that women should be conscripted for military service in wartime so that they could participate in "the privilege of killing, suffering, maiming, wasting, paralyzing, impoverishing, losing mental and physical vigor, in shoveling under the dead and themselves dying gloriously."[13]

Working to her limits as always, she barely maintained her own health until the November 1918 armistice, then took on the added stress and long hours of dealing with the great influenza epidemic that followed. Miraculously, she did not contract this killer strain of flu, but by the end of the year was laid low by a severe, undiagnosed infection.[14] Antibiotics had not been discovered yet, of course. The prescribed treatment was a series of painful irrigations of the sinus; Amelia submitted silently. During a long period of recuperation in Northampton, Massachusetts, under the watchful care of Amy and Muriel, she improved considerably.

Characteristically, because there was a strict family taboo against drawing attention to one's own problems, there is scant mention of this ordeal in Amelia's letters. Nonetheless, the infection would persist for the rest of her life, causing chronic pain. As a consequence, she would have to endure repeated surgical operations, two of them following her famous flights of 1932 and 1935.

Ironically, perhaps, Amelia's illness put her in the way of an opportunity that would prove to be of enormous value to her career. Forced to rest in Northampton but bored with doing nothing, she took a class in auto repair at nearby Smith College.[15] When she became a pilot, her knowledge of motors would give her a definite edge over the competition and make her as much at home among the airport grease monkeys as in the cockpit.

By the fall of 1919, she had recovered enough to become a medical student at Columbia University in New York City. Soon, despite her success in the wartime casualty wards, Amelia decided that she was not really interested in patient care as a profession.[16] She set her sights instead on scientific and medical research.[17] As one of her professors would recall much later, she had not changed her classroom ways since high school. Before he finished explaining to his class how to set up a particular mathematical equation, Amelia blurted out the solution but refused to explain how she had solved the problem without going through the conventional steps. Such undoubted brilliance would quite naturally attract the attention of her classmates, most of them male, but it was also clear that Amelia sought out such ways of setting herself apart.

It was not just the admiration of the crowd that would concern Amelia between the spring and fall terms of 1920. Perhaps for the first time, she fell in love.[18]

The setting was Los Angeles, where her father, having achieved a truce with his personal demons, had managed not only to sober up but also to establish a modestly successful private law practice. In yet another attempt to save her troubled marriage, Amy had joined him in a large rented house that spring. Because money was short, as always, the Earharts had decided to take in boarders, including a chemical-engineering graduate from Tufts named Sam Chapman.

Bright enough to match the sharp mind of the daughter visiting for summer break, the young man also shared Amelia's interest in tennis, swimming, and literature. He definitely did not, however, share her contempt for traditional views of marriage, and Amelia could not agree to give up her freedom to become a traditional wife. For that reason alone, it seems, the two lovers eventually parted, although they would remain friends until the day she vanished.

Perhaps, having loved her father to little avail, and having seen her parents become too wrapped up in their own personal turmoils to respond to the emotional needs of their daughters, Amelia had learned that love seldom deserves first priority in making one's plans. In any event, this time she was the one who chose not to respond. To fill whatever wounds love had inflicted throughout her life, she had learned very well to rely upon inner resources for nurturing her human needs for dignity and self-worth.

That summer was also memorable for giving the young woman her first real experience of flying.[19] Inspired by the incident with the "little red airplane" in Toronto, she had followed the "air circuses" of the day with fascination. After attending one such event in Long Beach with her father, she asked him to find out how much it cost to learn to fly. Edwin was understandably skeptical and concerned, but he stopped short of disapproval, and in fact made the arrangements.[20] The very next day, at Long Beach's Rogers Field, she went aloft for the first time.

"I went to California for a summer vacation," she would later say, "and found air meets, as distinct from wartime exhibitions, just beginning. I went to every one and finally one day . . . Frank Hawks [sic] took me on my first hop. He was then just a barnstorming pilot on the West Coast, unknown to the fame he later acquired. By the time I had got two or three hundred feet off the ground, I knew I had to fly."[21] Frank Hawkes, though little remembered today, became a prominent figure in West Coast aviation, the holder of many records in flying.

Undoubtedly, Amelia really did love flying for itself, but it is clear that other factors attracted her to the sport as well. A maverick, she enjoyed impressing people with the unusual things she could do better than anyone else, and not only in math class at Columbia. By going into yet another male-dominated field, she could both *épater les bourgeois* and also become an example to other women. Finally, she was just coming into her majority, a woman eager to get on with her own life and determine its course for herself. As a medical student, however, she was both financially dependent upon her parents and emotionally bound by her excessive sense of responsibility for them and their perennial difficulties. Flying offered her the promise, however illusory, of independence.

In reality, the immediate obstacle to her becoming an aviator was the old familiar family nemesis: lack of money. Lessons would cost $1,000, a huge sum in the 1920s, and Edwin, though his daughter did not hesitate to ask, could not possibly afford such an outlay. In fact, he now began actively to resist Amelia's scheme to learn to fly, but she was of course not to be deterred.[22] To earn part of the money, she landed a job with the telephone company, then persuaded her hapless father to pay her for helping out in his law office.[23]

With several weeks of salary in hand as a kind of down payment, she was able to strike a deal with Neta Snook, a crusty pioneer of women's aviation, who agreed to give her lessons on the installment plan. Amelia's course was set.[24]

CHAPTER THREE

Fame

> ... AE was something of a prima donna. She had a
> facade of being shy and humble, but she really had
> an ego, and she could be as tough as nails when the
> occasion required it. I got very fed up with her bull-
> headedness several times. ...
>
> —U.S. Navy Captain (later Admiral) Harry
> Manning, Earhart's occasional copilot/navigator[1]

Amelia cut her hair and began spending
weekends at the Kinner Field in southern
Los Angeles, where Snook ran her flying
school, and where Bert Kinner, a famous
pioneer of early aviation, invented and
built a small two-seat biplane known as the
Kinner Airster. Earhart quickly made herself at home, beginning her flight training in
a Canuck biplane. She acquired the essential components of a proper flying outfit
and was thereafter more often than not
seen dressed in trousers and a jacket, hov-
ering over the airplanes and engines alongside the pilots and mechanics.[2] Never

afraid to ask questions, she obtained much valuable instruction firsthand and free. (George Palmer Putnam's introduction to *Last Flight*, the "posthumous" collection of
Earhart's occasional pieces and flight log, captures this
quality memorably: "She was seldom happier, I think,
than when perched on a service-stand watching some ad-
justment of her beloved engines, or sprawled on the concrete tarmac observing experts wrestle with a troublesome
strut or dump valve. And probably as grimy as a grease
monkey.")

After some twenty hours of instruction, she made her
first solo flight as Neta and Muriel watched nervously
from the ground.[3] It was a moment that created far greater
distance between Amelia and her family than the five
thousand feet to which she climbed that day.

Next she became determined to have an airplane of her
own. Only six months after her first solo flight, and just
prior to her twenty-fourth birthday, Amelia was able to
put a down payment on a bright yellow Kinner Airster,
which she named *The Canary*.[4] Kinner's first design, it was
powered by a sixty-horsepower, three-cylinder Lawrence
radial. Characteristically, Earhart stubbornly ignored
Snook's warning that the aircraft was underpowered and
far less stable than the Canuck.[5]

Her father had rather vaguely agreed to provide the bal-
ance of the purchase price, but changed his mind. To pay
for *The Canary*, Amelia had to pool together all of her
savings, her sister, Muriel's savings, and some of the
money their mother had received from the sale of her
parents' house in Atchison.[6] Clearly, she was not going to
be deterred by her father, whose weakness had been
shown so vividly in his bouts with alcohol. (It should be
remembered that at that point neither Edwin nor anyone
else had reason to believe that Amelia's flight training was

anything more than expensive, perhaps frivolous, recreation.) She showed herself to be just as manipulative, stubborn, and possibly insensitive to the emotional needs and physical safety of others as she would be time and again when she felt someone stood between her and what she wanted.

And, even though she could not have known what she would eventually become, there seemed to be a pattern forming in her actions, an unconscious design. In October 1922, for example, at the Long Beach Airshow, she set an altitude record for women by climbing to fourteen thousand feet.[7] This absolutely pointless act brought her sudden notoriety. Much to the consternation of the more conservative and reserved members of her family, her lean, somewhat androgynous profile appeared in the Los Angeles newspapers.

But Amelia, unquestionably concerned with her image, knew exactly what she was doing. To reporters, she invariably came across as shy, modest, and a little embarrassed by all of the fuss and attention. The portrayal was partly true, but it is also clear that she had a gift for public relations and self-promotion long before the two terms came into popular usage.

Her quirky attire was part of the calculation, as suggested by Fred Goerner in his biography:

Amelia loved the role. She wore boots and khaki pants, with a scarf wrapped around her throat and folded inside a knee-length, leather flying jacket which had been properly "aged" with the right amount of grease and simulated wear. A leather helmet with goggles completed the uniform. The costume had a practical side. . . . But practicality had little to do with [it]. . . . She liked the girl she saw in the mirror. The image was daring, courageous, independent. In short, Amelia

Earhart found her identity as a flier, and she never relin-
quished it.[8]

As had been demonstrated back at Hyde Park High
School and Columbia Medical School, Earhart knew how
to draw attention to herself without seeming to do so deliberately. A loner, she apparently never shared her ambitious plans with anyone until her marriage years later to a
man who was a genius of promotion. But it is obvious that
she at least knew that she wanted to excel at something
women ordinarily did not do. From that point of view, it
was precisely the right time in history for her move into
aviation, and she took full advantage of the potential.

Not less important to the older daughter of the ill-fated
Earharts, flying carried her away from the daily travails of
her family's unsettled existence, and safely out of range of
intimacy and personal involvement. At age twenty-three,
all by herself in a Kinner biplane almost three miles up in
the air, she crossed a threshold that put her former existence forever behind her.

Still, she could not entirely escape the family troubles
that threatened to curtail her flying career. When Mrs.
Earhart's inheritance had dwindled down dangerously to
only $20,000, Amelia insisted that Edwin protect the
money by investing the entire amount in a gypsum mine.[9]
The same year she logged her altitude record, 1922, a flash
flood wiped out the mine, and with it the family's nest egg.
That was the end of any further educational plans for the
two daughters.

Amelia, with the help of a friend, Lloyd Royer, tried to
salvage something by operating a truck that survived the
mining venture. This enterprise soon folded. In the mean-
time, Royer fell in love with his spunky partner and proposed marriage, unsuccessfully, at least once in the early

part of 1923.[10] (Coincidentally, he would be employed as a design engineer at Lockheed Aircraft Corporation during the construction of the Electra in which Amelia was to disappear in the Pacific.)

By 1924, the Earharts finally separated for good, causing yet another interruption to their daughter's flying activities. Muriel had married and moved to Medford, Massachusetts, and Amelia felt responsible for helping their mother through an emotionally and financially difficult time. She sold The Canary, bought an equally bright yellow sports car, a Kissel, and drove her mother back east to live with Muriel and her husband, Albert Morrissey.

Remaining in the area to give her mother emotional support, Amelia began teaching English to foreign students in an extension program at the University of Massachusetts. Because the classes were held at various industrial towns around the state, her meager earnings were well nigh exhausted by travel expenses. In the spring of 1926, she became a social worker at Boston's Denison House, teaching English to the immigrant children residing there.[11] Evidently quite dedicated, she was soon promoted to be a resident. She was still working there in April 1928, when Hilton Railey, at the urging of George Palmer Putnam, head of the publishing house of G. P. Putnam's Sons, stopped by with an offer that would radically change her life, and his.[12]

A certain Mrs. Frederick (Amy) Guest, a Pittsburgh-born socialite who was married to a former British air minister, wanted to become the first woman to fly across the Atlantic. She determined to sponsor a flight in which she would participate as one of the crew. Once she bought a Fokker Trimotor seaplane from the internationally famous explorer Admiral Richard Byrd, however, her family stepped in and objected stridently. They well knew the somber roster of those who had tried and failed to make the trip. Mrs. Guest was forced to find a surrogate aviatrix.

Meanwhile, she had decided that the trip should be chronicled in a book, and had asked Admiral Byrd to introduce her to Putnam, who was quite taken with the idea. He had previously succeeded in getting Charles Lindbergh to write the story of his flight, which proved to be a big money-maker, and expected to wring even more revenue out of the adventures of the first woman to fly the Atlantic. As he would prove frequently in the coming years, Putnam had an uncanny feel for which aviation feats would generate the type of publicity that could produce a substantial financial fallout from testimonials, books, magazines, motion pictures, and product endorsements *ad infinitum*. Mrs. Guest's scheme was a pitchman's dream come true, but it lacked one crucial element: the woman to be the heroine. When she told Putnam she would have to back out, he looked around for a suitable replacement. His good friend Hilton Railey found Amelia.

So it was that the publisher sent Railey to seek out the social worker with a question to which there could be only one answer: "Would you be interested in becoming the first woman to fly across the Atlantic Ocean?"[13]

The whole project, as it would turn out, was fairly typical of the kinds of exploits Putnam would devise for Amelia in the future. In fact, he would gain the reputation, deserved or not, of being an enormously successful but less than entirely scrupulous promoter of her career.

But this first proposal was certainly in line with what Amelia considered to be her own interests. She accepted without a moment's hesitation. To her dismay, however, she learned that she would be participating only as a passenger. The pilot was to be Wilmer "Bill" Stultz, who had a serious alcohol problem.[14] A mechanic, Lou Gordon, would also be along for the flight.

On June 3, 1928, with the boozy Stultz at the controls and Earhart and Gordon as passengers, Mrs. Guest's Fokker, *Friendship*, lifted off shakily from Boston Harbor for Harbor Grace, Newfoundland. There the weather would delay the transatlantic flight for fourteen days. While the trio sat tensely waiting, Putnam and his friend Admiral Byrd continually forwarded weather reports and forecasts from New York City. Adding to the tension was competition from Mabel Boll, a nonpilot who had set her sights on being the first female to make the hop.[15] She and her pilots, the noted air corpsmen Oliver Le Boutillier and Arthur Argles, were also waiting for the weather to lift.[16] Still a third possible competitor caused Amelia to fret. Thea Rasche, a pilot, might take off at any time and lay claim to the title.[17] To make matters worse, and in fact almost impossible, Stultz was drinking so heavily that the entire enterprise seemed doubtful, no matter what the weather.[18]

But when weather and sea conditions finally turned favorable on June 17, Earhart and Gordon decided to pour their pilot into the cockpit of the Fokker, even though he was suffering the ill effects of his latest drinking bout. Stultz came round enough to aim the *Friendship* across Trepassey Bay and open the throttle.

Unfortunately, the big seaplane, with its 220-horsepower Wright J-5 Whirlwind engine was severely underpowered for the weight it was carrying. Although the fuel load was at an absolute minimum for the long flight, it was still so heavy that the aircraft could not break free of the surface of the harbor. No sooner would it approach flying speed than a wave splashed up by the foundering pontoons would drench an engine, causing it to sputter and lose power.

After three abortive attempts to take off, the team de-cided to reduce the fuel quantity even more, down to a dangerously low level of seven hundred gallons. Finally, after a "desperate takeoff run of almost three miles," the *Friendship* rose reluctantly into the air. Stultz managed to coax the ship into a shallow climb and set it on a ragged course for the coast of England.[19]

In twenty hours and forty minutes of flying, the adven-turers would encounter all types of weather and nearly exhaust their fuel. But they would win the new record, after all, and Stultz was able to ease the Fokker smoothly onto the waters of Burry Port, Wales.[20] The first woman to make a transatlantic flight had never even touched the controls, but Amelia Earhart's aviation career was back on track nonetheless. She started flying again as soon as she returned home from England.

The very next year, 1929, Putnam finagled Lockheed Aircraft Company into lending Earhart the firm's power-ful new single-engine Vega.[21] She used it to capture a new women's speed record, peaking at just over 184 miles an hour. In Detroit on June 25, 1930, she set two speed rec-ords, the first for a hundred kilometers, the second for a hundred kilometers while carrying a five-hundred-kilo-gram payload.

Also in 1929, Putnam jettisoned his wife, Dorothy Bin-ney Putnam, and proposed marriage to the young woman he was in effect managing as a commercial property.[22] Ear-hart, ten years younger than the entrepreneur, rejected this and the following five proposals, but her resistance apparently weakened as his promotion of her flying career and creation of her public image continued to prove so unerringly successful. On February 7, 1931, three years after their first meeting and the transatlantic record, Ame-lia Earhart and George Palmer Putnam II were married in Noank, Connecticut.[23]

It is fair to say both that Amelia deliberately put herself in the hands of a promotional genius and that Putnam recognized she was as well packaged an article as he could ever hope to market. Supremely self-confident, he made it his business to know everyone worth knowing in the arts, politics, and industry. His young wife was to be surrounded by the luminaries of the day, from celebrity journalist Ben Hecht to the prince of Wales, from Eugene Vidal (director of the Bureau of Air Commerce) to humorist Robert Benchley—tall cotton for a girl from Kansas. Putnam was a fast-talking deal-maker known for being able to see his chances and seize them, with time left over for unabashed self-aggrandizement. He was said to have an ego so large it could be seen only from the air.

Not surprisingly, he was disliked by quite a few, including many of Amelia's friends and her mother. But he was also widely respected for his very real accomplishments, including the continuing success of his prestigious publishing house and the fact that he had written several books. With easy authority, he controlled a world in which Amelia wanted to play a part, a world of money, access, power, and, above all, publicity. Perhaps, too, marriage to the somewhat older Putnam provided her with a substitute father figure, for the pathetic Edwin Earhart had died recently from cancer.

Still, Amelia may have had some misgivings about the man she had resisted for so many months. In a famous note she presented to the bridegroom on their wedding day, she laid down a condition to the marriage pact: "Let me go in one year if we find no happiness together."[24]

In fact, such happiness apparently did bless the union, at least to some degree, for the independent Amelia did not avail herself of this escape clause. Even so, there would be some speculation, after her disappearance in the Pacific, that she had simply contrived a way of escaping from Putnam, his manipulations, and the prying public eye. It would seem, in other words, that the marriage never quite rang true for many observers.

Whatever the truth about the relationship, the young bride continued to do what she did best. It was on April 8, only two months after the nuptials, that she broke two altitude records for the autogiro in the same day.[25] She was determined to become the first person to fly one of these rare contraptions from coast to coast. Characteristically, Putnam arranged for the Beech-Nut Packing Company to sponsor the attempt, and even to buy his wife a PCA-2 autogiro from Pitcairn Aircraft Company.[26]

Amelia expected little competition for this dubious achievement, which involved an aircraft that would become the Edsel of aviation. When she landed in Los Angeles, however, she was surprised (and her husband outraged) to learn that another pilot had captured the record just the week before. Undaunted, Amelia hopped back in her autogiro and headed homeward, determined to become the first person to make the round trip.

Along the way, she gave a demonstration flight at a fair in Abilene, Texas, that ended in near-disaster. On takeoff, a flailing rotor blade struck a light standard and fractured, sending slivers of metal flying around the crowded fairgrounds as the autogiro self-destructed right in front of the horrified spectators. Miraculously, neither Amelia nor any of the bystanders was injured. A replacement craft was rushed out from the Pitcairn factory, and Earhart completed her record flight back to New York without further incident.[27]

Soon after she returned the autogiro to the manufacturer, a company pilot crashed it during a landing attempt. It was repaired well enough for Amelia to give a demonstration flight at an air show near Detroit later in the year, but she, too, smashed up on landing. This time, the air-

craft was totaled. Thus ended Earhart's dangerous flirta-
tion with the bizarre and unpredictable autogiro.

Much more conventionally, she bought a red Lockheed
Vega and set out from Harbor Grace, Newfoundland, on
May 20, 1932, to fly the Atlantic again, this time alone.[28] It
was a trip that underscored the perils of flight in the days
before the invention of anti- and deicing equipment.
There were several violent storms, and ice accumulated to
threatening levels on the wings and other parts of the airplane structure. At one point, there was so much ice that
the flow of air over the wings was finally impeded. The
Vega stalled and spun downward some three thousand
feet, nearly striking the water, before the warmer air of the
lower elevations melted the ice. At the other extreme, an
inflight fire caused by a broken exhaust manifold came
just as close to ending the flight in disaster.

She would later write about this exhausting trip with
her familiar clarity, wry humor, and frankness:

> Looking back, there are less cheering recollections of that
> night over the Atlantic. Of seeing, for instance, the flames
> lick through the exhaust collector ring and wondering, in a
> detached way, whether one would prefer drowning to incin-
> eration. Of the five hours of storm, during black midnight,
> when I kept right side up by instruments alone, buffeted
> about as I never was before. Of much besides, not the least
> the feeling of fine loneliness and of realization that the ma-
> chine I rode was doing its best and required from me the best
> I had.[29]

At last, after a trip of fourteen hours and fifty-six minutes, Amelia reached Londonderry, Ireland, thus becoming the first woman to fly solo across the Atlantic.

She was now an international sensation. New York wel-
comed her back home with a tumultuous ticker-tape pa-

rade, and she was honored with the Distinguished Flying Cross, the first woman to receive this rare and highly coveted award for civilian aviators. As famous as the most famous, including Charles Lindbergh, who had been the most beloved human being in the world since his solo crossing of the Atlantic in 1927, she was tagged by journalists with that nickname she despised, "Lady Lindy."

But she did not rest on her impressive laurels. Later in the year, she set a woman's nonstop transcontinental speed record by covering the 2,478 miles between Los Angeles and Newark, New Jersey, in nineteen hours, five minutes. She beat her record on the same route in July 1933, with a time of seventeen hours, seven and a half minutes.

She set her sights even higher. On December 24, 1934, her red-and-gold Vega was hauled aboard the Matson liner SS *Lurline* for shipment to Hawaii.[30] A group of businessmen in the island territory, the Hawaiian Sugar Planters Association, had announced a $10,000 prize for the first person to fly solo across the Pacific from Hawaii to the U.S. mainland. But aboard the *Lurline* with his wife and her technical adviser Paul Mantz, Putnam told the press only that Amelia was sailing to Honolulu in order to make some flights around the islands and give a series of lectures. He did not mention that she would be attempting to set a record, or that it was he who had convinced the sugar producers to put up the prize money.

Even before the Putnams arrived in Honolulu, however, the publicity began to turn sour, threatening a public-relations disaster. Business rivals of the sponsors circulated the rumor that she had been hired by the sugar growers to use her considerable influence to lobby the U.S. Congress for lower sugar tariffs. In fact, the sponsors were definitely interested in gaining some advantage in their campaign to defeat pending legislation, the proposed

Jones-Costigan Sugar Control Act. Faced with the prospect that their scheme would blow up in their faces because of the bad publicity, the alarmed sponsors considered canceling the flight altogether.

Amelia confronted them forthwith in a meeting at the Royal Hawaiian Hotel. "Gentlemen, there is the aroma of cowardice in this air," she said sternly. "You know as well as I this [rumor] is trash, but if you can be intimidated, it might as well be true. Whether you live in fear or defend your integrity is your decision; I have made mine. This week I will fly to California."[31]

She went ahead with final preparations for the record attempt. In addition to thoroughly testing the Vega's engine and radio equipment, she had the five passenger seats removed in order to install 520-gallon fuel tanks. Despite this large amount, she and Mantz estimated that she would have fewer than fifty gallons left when she reached California. Whether she would land in Oakland or Los Angeles would depend upon the wind.

She secured the appropriate authorization for the flight from the Department of Commerce, which at the time held jurisdiction over all matters involving U.S. aviation. Permission was granted, with the stipulation that she establish two-way radio communication with the U.S. mainland and maintain it throughout the flight.[32]

Her first attempts to comply with this restriction were frustrating. She arranged to have WKFI, a Los Angeles commercial-broadcast radio station, commissioned to provide the radio link. Hour after hour on January 10, Earhart, Mantz, and mechanic Ernie Tissot tried in vain to establish the contact. But, depending on the time of day and the atmospheric conditions, one or the other end of the transoceanic connection would fail. Officials from Commerce and the navy worried that Amelia's transmitter might be inadequate to broadcast such a long distance; in fact, it was the WKFI transceivers that were unable either to establish or to maintain contact.

Throughout the day, the Earhart team's frustrated radio transmissions were picked up by Walter B. McMenamy, a Los Angeles radio operator who was one of the few people on the West Coast with a radio transceiver powerful enough to maintain the government-required radio link. He just happened to be home and became amused, as he would recall for me decades later, at out-receiving the WKFI pros. More seriously, the much-touted "miracle of radio," as the phrase went in those halcyon early days of the medium, was about to suffer a humiliating fiasco, while the world watched. Seeing this, McMenamy loaded his equipment in the trunk of his car and drove down to the radio station; he had little difficulty persuading the rather embarrassed station manager to let him try his luck in reaching Amelia. He succeeded, and set Earhart's plans back on course.[33]

From the time she took off from Wheeler Field late in the afternoon of January 11, McMenamy would talk to Amelia throughout the eighteen-hour, fifteen-minute flight. This was in itself a record, if a little-noticed one, for hers was the first civil aircraft to carry and use a two-way radio. An entry in her log helps capture the moment:

It was just five o'clock as I passed over Makapuu Point, the last island outpost on my course. Shortly afterward, I let down my radio antenna and sent my first message, something like this: "Flying 6,000 feet through scattered clouds, temperature outside 50 degrees. Everything okay."[34]

Earhart used her radio not only to communicate with McMenamy, her official contact, but also to talk to Putnam, live, over a commercial radio station. This was, to be sure, first and foremost one of her husband's publicity stunts, but it also marked an important advance in aviation communications.[35]

The flight was wearing and sometimes perilous. Later, Earhart would admit that she had been lost part of the time, even as she continued to broadcast her position throughout the night. But she achieved her goal, ending her twenty-four-hundred-mile journey at Oakland. There, alerted by her radio transmissions and the attendant reportage, a tumultuous crowd of cheering fans greeted this dashing heroine. Newsreel cameras recorded her landing. President Roosevelt cabled congratulations.

Her celebrity even brighter now, Earhart was sought as a public speaker, but not just to talk about flying. No one had been more successful in an endeavor that had been portrayed popularly as requiring superhuman qualities; she was therefore expected to speak about the role of women in a male-dominated world, as well as about the dominant social and political issues of the day.

She took every chance to deliver her message to women: Don't be stopped; do whatever it is you want to do in life. Women are equal in ability to men; they can and should pursue challenging careers outside the kitchen and bedroom.

At the same time, with her husband's help and guidance, Amelia took full advantage of her tremendous commercial value. The money flowed in from the speaking engagements, magazine articles, product endorsements, and licensing agreements for the use of her name on everything from children's toys to luggage.

Of course, Putnam was easily a millionaire before he met Amelia, well accustomed to a life of comfort and privilege. The couple had homes on both coasts, in Rye, New York, and Hollywood, California. Amelia not only flew the finest available aircraft but also indulged herself with one of the most daring and expensive automobiles of the day, a $5,500 Cord Sportsman convertible. The Putnams combined luxury with constant excitement, making them the envy of the masses who glimpsed their adventures in newsreels, magazines, or occasionally the front pages of newspapers.

With Putnam, moreover, Amelia found herself enjoying the kind of riches that money alone can never buy. Because of his many and varied social, business, and political contacts, the pair hobnobbed often with captains of industry, film idols, heirs to great fortunes, and heads of state. President and Mrs. Roosevelt entertained them at the White House; abroad, they were quite literally received by "the crowned heads of Europe."

Fame also gave Amelia a convenient buffer against any emotionally wearing involvement with her family. She maintained a distant if completely correct relationship with her mother and Muriel that gradually evolved into a nearly one-sided routine of brief letters, mailed gifts, and money sent to pay off bills and mortgages. She rarely visited them. Often, gifts of money to Amy came with reprimands about what Amelia called "the family problem"— that is, her mother's financial imprudence.[36] Amelia's assumption of fiscal responsibility for her estranged family won her a reputation for generosity among even her more distant relatives.

In this way, perhaps, she dealt with the two themes that had always marked her unhappy family history—the fear of failing like her weak and incompetent father, the need to avoid the kind of intimacy that would lead to rejection of her love. In her late thirties, she was enjoying the flowering of years of superhuman effort to succeed at any cost. Surely the life she led proved that she was no failure, and, in place of love, she could settle for the admiration of millions.

There was a price to pay, of course. To keep that admiration fresh and fervent, to remain center stage, Amelia Earhart had to keep coming up with yet another dangerous challenge, yet another unprecedented achievement. Not long after the triumph of the Honolulu-Oakland flight, she took a hard look at the shrinking number of possible major aviation feats still unclaimed in the record books. Of course, whatever she chose would have to be even more daring than the Honolulu-Oakland flight— much more spectacular and dangerous. Characteristically, she decided to take the greatest aeronautical challenge of them all, a venture so daunting that no one had even made the attempt. She would fly around the world at the equator.

CHAPTER FOUR

Spy?

... a system of world-wide contacts has been worked out which will parallel the track of her flight around the Equator, adding immeasurably to her safety.

—*Los Angeles Times*, March 10, 1937

As might be expected, Earhart began preparations for her aerial circumnavigation of the globe by calling upon the network of technical advisers, mechanics, aircraft engineers, navigation experts, and other assistants who had helped her in the past.

To take a significant example, she called upon Walter McMenamy to help arrange for the installation of the necessary radio gear in her plane, as well as to establish a worldwide network of radio operators to monitor her flight and report her progress to newspapers and commercial radio stations.[1] McMenamy, flattered and thrilled at the chance to help Amelia Earhart again, accepted gladly. Over the following year, he succeeded in both assignments. He provided her with state-of-the-art radio equipment and arranged to have it properly installed in her new twin-engine Lockheed Electra monoplane. He also set up an intercontinental network of radio operators to cover her flight over some of the world's most isolated regions. His team for this effort included Karl E. Pierson, chief engineer for the Patterson Radio Company, along with Joseph Gurr and Guy Dennis, both active amateur radio enthusiasts who owned and operated the latest in long-range radio transceivers.

These men and others involved in the network belonged to the Radio Relay League, a worldwide organization of radio operators dedicated to advancing the use of shortwave radio as a means of communication. For the time, their task was daunting: to provide en-route communications that would ensure the safety of the flight, to relay Earhart's messages back home, to obtain weather reports and forecasts and forward them in good time, and to provide a conduit to the journalists everywhere. McMenamy and Pierson would coordinate the operation from a base station on Beacon Hill near Los Angeles, where radio reception was optimal.

Perhaps the idea of the network does not seem all that exciting or innovative in an age when communication is a virtual blizzard of information from competing media. In the late 1930s, however, the "magical" developments in radio were just as enthralling to the public as the daring achievements of civil aviation. And just as difficult to believe. On March 10, 1937, the *Los Angeles Times* ran a story about McMenamy's radio network that suggests something of the public fascination. The reporter's enthusiasm also offers some historical ironies:

TIMES TO KEEP IN TOUCH WITH AMELIA BY RADIO SHORT
WAVE STATIONS TO GIVE COMPLETE REPORTS ON FLYER'S
PROGRESS AROUND THE GLOBE

Through the magic of short wave radio, Amelia Earhart plans to maintain contact with her Los Angeles radio base and *The Times* while in the air on her 27,000-mile flight around the world.

From the moment the intrepid woman flyer takes off she will be in almost constant contact communications with radio amateurs.

Those dramatic moments that come to every flyer on pioneering treks over trackless wastes of ocean and strange uninhabited lands will be depicted from the air by the flyer herself over the ether waves.

Even the pulse beats of her motors may be heard by Los Angeles men with their ears covered by phones while they keep watch on her journey.

Not only will Miss Earhart's own personal story of her flight appear exclusively in *The Times* in Southern California—her hour-to-hour conversations with her radio base will be logged by amateurs in cooperation with *The Times*.

Every known device of science has been engaged to make Miss Earhart's flight a success. And through local radio amateurs a system of world-wide contacts has been worked out which will parallel the track of her flight around the Equator, adding immeasurably to her safety.

Manning the key station in Los Angeles will be Guy H. Dennis, owner of amateur station W6NNR at 1195 Crenshaw Boulevard; Walter B. McMenamy, of 749 Burnside Avenue, and Karl E. Pierson, of 1171 Montecito Drive.

The Dennis station is described as one of the most efficient amateur stations in the West, with a range encircling the globe.

Through the cooperation of Emmett R. Patterson, president of the Patterson Radio Company, the station will employ an entirely new type of Los Angeles–made short wave receiver designed by Pierson, who is chief engineer for the Patterson concern. It is known as the PR-15.

Miss Earhart and her navigator will rely on the Los Angeles men to maintain communication with her while in flight and relay messages to amateurs all along her route. Hourly schedules of intercommunication have been arranged and *The Times* will be supplied with the logs.

Operators of four other amateur stations, W6BGH, W6ALJ, W6CU, and W6CQK, have agreed to stand by and relieve the operators of W6NNR during the long period that Miss Earhart will be flying.

George Palmer Putnam, husband of Miss Earhart and manager of her flight, said that the radio tie-up with McMenamy and Dennis is a tribute to their valued work in maintaining communication with Miss Earhart on her flight from Honolulu. They also maintained communication with the Pan Am Clipper ships on the pioneering flights across the Pacific (1935) and with navigators of stratosphere balloons in recent years.

Amateur stations around the globe near the Equator will assist Miss Earhart through the local radio station. On the first leg of the flight, amateurs assisting will be Dr. Ferris W. Thompson, and William A. McCartney, Honolulu; Yau F. Lum of Howland Island in the South Pacific; F. W. Nolan, Brisbane, Australia, and Jacques Berlant, at New York City. The latter will maintain contact with Miss Earhart's New York headquarters.

Other short wave relay points will pick up Miss Earhart along her route and serve as guiding beacons to the flyer in remote places.[2]

Amelia's goals included the generation of enormous amounts of publicity, of course; such is the nature of any record-breaking attempt. For that reason, the media link was of paramount importance in the initial planning of her flight. As she herself admitted, many of her records brought no important advances in aviation, science, or society. Like an attempt to jump the Grand Canyon on a motorcycle today, they were a means to an end, a vehicle for attracting the attention of the masses. Her exploits had made Earhart a media superstar; press access to the progress of her latest flight was considered as essential to its success as fuel and oil for the Electra.

More than in any other time before or since, aviation record-setting was great theater in the 1930s. By 1937, Earhart was its biggest star, now surpassing even Lindbergh. Behind the scenes, of course, Putnam continued hustling her career assiduously, as he had since they first met in Boston. Quite simply, he viewed the public persona known to the world as Amelia Earhart as a money-making machine.

Apart from the fame and the fortune, however, there was a third element to Earhart's achievement that would be completely recognized and understood only in the highest echelons of government. She was, in fact, the only person in the country who could render a particular service, because of a unique conjunction of politics, destiny, skill, and equipment. As the world tuned in, she was going to fly to the far corners of the globe in one of the fastest, most sophisticated aircraft available. Moreover, as the famous civilian heroine Amelia Earhart, she enjoyed a precious commodity—the freedom to go anywhere, including places where the U.S. government was barred.

So it was that, in the midst of the publicity barrage for the upcoming flight, high-level officials in the Roosevelt administration, including the president himself, had the seeds of an idea. At the time, navy, State Department, and White House personnel had been casting about for any possible way of gaining even the smallest early advantage in the conflict looming inevitably in the Pacific. Amelia's decision to fly along the equator was perfectly, if unknowingly, timed for them.

Perhaps the government's idea, in its final form, took some time to develop. Certainly Earhart was merely a famous civilian asking a favor in 1936, when her husband requested that the navy help her conduct an air-to-air refueling operation over Midway Island in the Pacific. But Roosevelt's swift response was unprecedented. In a handwritten note to the chief of naval operations, he ordered, "Do what we can and contact Putnam."[3] Admiral William D. Leahy secretly made the arrangements, although the navy was somewhat reluctant at first. They required that she obtain training in the new technique, without offering to train her themselves, and insisted that she pay the cost of the refueling aircraft, the personnel involved, and the fuel, estimated at just over $1,000.[4]

From this point onward, increasingly strong links were forged between the U.S. government and the Earhart world-flight operation. Quite possibly, then, it was Amelia's initial request that inspired the president to consider the various ways in which her unique project could be used to military advantage. Certainly this would have been completely in character for the wily FDR, who rarely missed a chance to apply his remarkable creativity and fondness for intrigue.

Whatever the genesis of the behind-the-scenes plan, the secret air-to-air refueling mission, which would have been risky, was soon scuttled for an alternative scheme. Roosevelt decided to use the flight as a ruse to develop an airfield on Howland Island, part of the Line Islands group, along with Baker and Jarvis islands.[5] The islands in the chain were considered to be a potentially vital front line of defense, since they are virtually the only landmasses between Hawaii and the Marshall Islands, then held by the Japanese. Howland itself lay precisely on a line between Hawaii and Melanesia and to Australia beyond. The presi-

dent was astounded to learn that the U.S. did not technically own Howland or, in fact, any of the surrounding
islands in this region of rapidly increasing strategic importance. Such other strategic outposts as Wake and Midway
islands were under U.S. control and were being developed
by Pan American Airways, though strictly for civilian use.
These holdings were hundreds of miles north of Howland, however.

It is important to remember that war had already broken out in the Pacific. Since early in 1931, the Japanese
had been inexorably expanding their frontier, island by
island. Deeply troubled by these conquests, but hampered
politically in preparing defenses for U.S. interests in the
area, Roosevelt covertly set about to claim and colonize
the three Line Islands, then build airfields on each.[6]

A series of secret memoranda laid down the logistical
and diplomatic groundwork for pursuing these aims, beginning with an extensive confidential report and recommendation from Secretary of State Cordell Hull on February 18, 1936:

> Referring to your confidential memorandum of October
> 16, 1935 . . . concerning certain islands in the Pacific, includ-
> ing Jarvis, Howland and Baker Islands, it is believed that it
> would be desirable to place these islands by Executive Order
> under the administration of one of the Departments of the
> Government, possibly the Interior Department.
> Between March 25 and April 1, 1935, the *Itasca* landed
> several Americans (Hawaiians) on each of the three islands,
> and they have been continuously occupied since then. . . .
> [NOTE: This "colonization" was the subject of another secret
> memo to the president from Rex Martin, director of Air
> Commerce, on April 8, 1935.]
> . . . In view of all the circumstances in the case I think that
> an Executive Order could be issued placing these islands

under the jurisdiction of one of the Departments of the Government without first communicating in the matter with the British Government.[7]

What the honorable secretary of state was suggesting to the president of the United States was, in effect, that the nation quietly seize the islands, which had long been claimed by the British, and peremptorily lay claim to them in the hope that the executive order would carry its own weight and the Brits would not notice precisely what had occurred.

FDR responded the day after Hull wrote the memorandum:

> I entirely approve an Executive Order placing these Islands under the Interior Department. Will you speak with the Secretary of the Interior about it and have the necessary Order prepared?[8]

The scheme worked. Shortly after the executive order was issued and transfer of jurisdiction to Interior was completed, the Coast Guard cutter *William J. Duane* sailed from Honolulu to Howland, loaded with material and workers to begin construction of an airfield. As far as the public knew, of course, the project was being undertaken entirely as a courtesy to the civilian heroine Amelia Earhart.

Consider the dimensions of this taxpayer-supported "courtesy" for someone viewed in some circles as little more than a daredevil stunt flyer. The very landing on Howland Island was a major undertaking, to say nothing of the work that lay ahead, for there was no lagoon or landing area. Because the *Duane* could get no closer than a quarter of a mile from the shore, the equipment had to be brought on pontoons through the heavy surf crashing over treacherous reefs and shoals. Despite these daunting conditions, the crew hauled up an impressive array of equipment: two five-ton tractors, a farm-type harrow, a concrete-and-steel roller, matlocks, axes, plows, cane knives, a field kitchen, floodlamps, radio transmitting and receiving equipment, food, water, and many other items.

What faced them then was a charmless spit of land half a mile wide and a mile and a half long, covered with an estimated thirty thousand tons of guano. Whatever the problems, however, the crew hastily completed an airstrip that was said to have the best runways and approaches of any landing field in the world. Ironically, the claim has never been tested. To this day, although three impacted coral runways remain as firm and perfectly smooth as asphalt (the longest a mile long), no airplane has ever touched down on the airfield at Howland.

This remarkable construction job marked the beginning of the U.S. government's involvement in Earhart's flight, as well as the first preparations in the Pacific in anticipation of war. There is simply no other explanation or justification for such an unprecedented collaboration between government and a private undertaking.

But it was only the beginning. From then on, the Roosevelt administration and the navy took an increasingly active interest in her plans, and a web of secrecy began to weave itself ever more tightly around the flight and the flyer.

Coincidentally, Amelia's best-laid plans would go awry in a way that would play into the hands of government strategists.

On March 17, 1937, the usual spring rain had been falling continuously on the West Coast for about a week. At

Oakland Airport, Amelia Earhart and her crew waited for a break in the weather. Hawaii was planned as the first stop on a westward circumnavigation.[9]

When, late in the afternoon, a few rays of sun pierced through the overcast, U.S. Navy personnel rolled Earhart's plane out of the hangar and prepared it for flight. The sleek silver Lockheed Model 10E Electra was named by Lockheed, prophetically, after the Lost Star of the Pleiades. The latest thing in aviation, a pilot's dream plane, it had been presented to Amelia by her husband on her thirty-ninth birthday, July 24, 1936.[10]

It was a generous gift that the wealthy publisher and pitchman could well afford; however, as sources from Amelia herself to an official of Purdue University would indicate, he did not in fact put up the money. A. A. Potter, dean emeritus of Purdue's Department of Engineering (where Earhart had been a visiting faculty lecturer), provided a partial explanation:

> Miss Earhart's plane was purchased for her in the interest of national defense. The money was channeled through two private individuals to the Purdue Research Foundation. The monies, in the amount of $80,000 (equal to over $1 million in 1980 dollars) . . . were then given to Miss Earhart so she could make the actual purchase of the aircraft. Among her tasks was the development of direction finding equipment for the U.S. military.[11]

In other words, Earhart was being given the aircraft for "scientific purposes." But the key word here is "channeled," clearly indicating that Purdue did not fund the purchase outright.

Who did pay for the aircraft? It is possible that the money was somehow provided by the government, or that Lockheed Aircraft Corporation never actually sold the airplane. The original bill of sale (Lockheed registration number N16020) indicates that the Electra was transferred to an individual identified only as "Livingston." By coincidence or not, Amelia did have a close friend, Clara Livingston, also a pilot, who was living in Puerto Rico at the time. The bill of sale was not made public, however, and consequently no one investigated what it might actually mean.[12]

From several indications, including Earhart's own imprecise explanation, it can be inferred that the money was provided by a group of wealthy "philanthropists." These included the "two private individuals" referred to in Dean Potter's statement: Vincent Bendix, founder and chairman of the Bendix Corporation, and J. K. Lilly, the multimillionaire head of the J. K. Lilly conglomerate.[13] Joining with them was industrialist Floyd Odlum, owner of a vast cosmetics fortune, aviation enthusiast, and fervent patriot. He was also the husband of Amelia's best friend, the accomplished aviator Jacqueline Cochran.

Perhaps these benefactors would have good reason to keep their involvement secret, no matter what the intended purpose of the airplane. With millions of people destitute in the continuing Great Depression, the size of the gift might have been portrayed as frivolous extravagance or arrogant insensitivity. In any event, the decision to channel the funds through Purdue, whoever actually provided them, assured that the Electra was given the imprimatur of scientific research. In those more innocent times, few would have leapt to the conclusion that "pure" research could be linked with military goals.

But, in truth, Earhart would begin her round-the-world trip in the Electra with the active and visible participation of the U.S. Navy. When the decision was made to lift off from Oakland at last, she was driven to her plane in a navy staff car. Beforehand, her technical adviser Paul Mantz, who would also serve as copilot for this flight, performed the usual copilot's chores of preflight inspection and checking of the engines by running them up. (He had decided at the last minute to go along for this first leg of the attempt, so that he could meet with his fiancée in Honolulu.) Mantz had been joined by the two navigators for the flight, Fred Noonan and Navy Captain Harry Manning.

When Earhart was ready, she pointed the nose down the runway and eased the throttles forward. After a ground run of slightly more than eighteen hundred feet, the seven-ton Electra rose and climbed out over the Golden Gate into clearing skies.

The Pacific was a much different ocean then, as one incident illustrates. About an hour into the flight, according to Amelia's log, she sighted a Pan American Clipper flying near. She was later astonished to learn that, despite hundreds of hours of flying over the Pacific, no Clipper crew had ever sighted another flying boat in the air.[14] Pan Am had begun mail service on the route only two years before; passenger service had not been offered until 1936. In effect, the spacious skies above the broad ocean were virtually deserted.

Another difference is that the Pacific took much, much longer to navigate back then. When Earhart landed at Wheeler Field early on March 18, after a smooth and uneventful flight, she had set a new record for the transpacific route: fifteen hours and forty-seven minutes. Today's tourist makes the same trip in about a third of this record time. In further contrast, travelers in the 1930s spent days getting from the U.S. to Hong Kong on the Pan Am Clippers. Even surface travel took longer than today—passenger ships were slower by weeks, freighters by months.

The day after their arrival, Mantz ferried the Electra

from Wheeler to nearby Luke Field, an Army Air Corps facility on Ford Island, which is in the middle of Pearl Harbor. The paved runway at Luke would facilitate the takeoff of the plane when it was heavily loaded down for the next leg with about nine hundred gallons of fuel. So far as is known, no one questioned the propriety, much less the legality, of a civil airplane pilot's using a military airfield in cooperation with military personnel.

From the field, over the masts and turrets of warships tied up along Battleship Row, the Earhart team could see clearly what was commonly known as "the Japanese smokescreen," the permanent cloud that tops the steep, emerald-colored mountain ridge that forms the spine of the island of Oahu. The sardonic nickname shows that, even then, the men stationed at Pearl fully expected Japanese aircraft to use this cloud one day for concealing their approach to attack the harbor.

Significantly, Earhart's nearly new Electra made a sharp contrast with the military aircraft at Luke. They were the best the country had, but most were at least ten years obsolete. Still, they had remained in excellent condition. The army could not afford to fly them frequently enough to wear them out. Nor, because of the same budgetary constraints, could the pilots there (and elsewhere throughout the Army Air Corps) easily get in enough flying time to maintain their basic proficiency.

(The country was woefully unprepared even three years later. On September 27, 1940, FDR told Army Chief of Staff General George C. Marshall that the British desperately needed bombers from the U.S. General Marshall had the unpleasant duty of informing the president that only forty-nine of the planes were in inventory for our own defense. Moreover, the Boeing Airplane Company could produce no more than approximately thirty-five per year. This was the state of affairs in an industry that, by war's end, would be producing close to a hundred thousand aircraft annually.[15])

On March 20, the trio of Earhart, Noonan, and Captain Manning were ready to continue to the next announced stop, Howland Island. A small crowd of soldiers and sailors gathered to watch the planned departure toward the west. Within minutes, however, Earhart's flight plans—and, indeed, her life—would change dramatically and forever.

Well into the ground run during takeoff, a scant few seconds before it would have become airborne, the Electra suddenly swerved and began a "groundloop," a general loss of the directional control necessary to make a straight track down the runway. The landing gear folded up under the fuselage, and the plane screamed to a sickening halt.

What had happened? Several years later, Manning graphically recalled this potentially fatal event:

> Amelia was responsible for the crash in Honolulu. I was flying copilot. She overcorrected for sway with too much left rudder, so we headed for the water. Then she overcorrected to the right, and we were headed for the hangars. There was nothing I could do about it. I felt the gear going, and I was ready to die. Sparks were coming up everywhere. Gas was all over the place. We were all just damned lucky it didn't catch fire.[16]

Shaken but unhurt, Earhart, Noonan, and Manning climbed out and inspected the damage. In addition to the collapse of the landing gear, the propeller blades were bent aft and the engine mounts badly twisted. Meanwhile, back in Oakland, Putnam had just heard the announcement of his wife's impending departure on the radio when the telephone rang. A wire-service reporter asked, "Have you heard? They crashed. The ship's in flames." Putnam was nearly overcome. It was several minutes before he learned the truth.[17]

In *Last Flight*, Earhart attributes the crash to an overload of the right shock strut, a large, shock-absorbing device attached to the landing gear.[18] Ordinarily, that would have been a sensible surmise, since any mechanical component is subject to failure. In the case of this particular Lockheed Electra, however, such failure was not highly likely.

According to documents obtained from the Federal Aviation Administration in 1982, Lockheed's engineers, fully aware that the plane would be used for long-distance endurance flights that required maximum fuel loads, had installed the strongest landing-gear components then available. Even with nine hundred gallons of fuel aboard, the Electra was about a ton (250 gallons) below its maximum fuel capacity, and therefore well below its maximum takeoff weight. It had often taken off with a heavier load, as it would have been required to do later in this flight, particularly on the much longer leg planned from Howland to Lae, New Guinea.

On the other hand, the shock strut could have collapsed because of an acceleration overload caused by an abrupt swerve, even with a plane below maximum takeoff weight. Manning's and Earhart's versions of the accident, in other words, would thus jibe; if indeed she did "overcorrect to the right," she could have caused an acceleration overload. Other theories proposed for the mishap have suggested a deliberate "groundloop"—to buy time for some reason, or even as sabotage—but we will probably never know the precise truth.

Whatever the cause, the result was that the record attempt was delayed until the Electra could be repaired or replaced. Time was a critical factor, for some of the complicated logistics and other arrangements still in place for the flight would be difficult to maintain. These included the worldwide radio network, the special government clearances for landing, and the provisioning of remote landing facilities.[19]

Radio communications were especially critical, for two reasons: the slight additional margin of safety, and the press coverage that could reap huge financial benefits later. Earhart would of course need to stay informed of the weather ahead of her, and also have some means of radioing her position if she crashed or had to make an unplanned landing. In truth, accurate weather information would still be minimal, given that there were few if any facilities for collecting and disseminating meteorological data along many equatorial stretches of ocean, desert, and rain forest. Still, the radio network could offer a slight edge, in terms of relaying general weather forecasts; they might also be able to help if she needed to have a repairman or a replacement part available at her next stop. As for the publicity machine, radio would be invaluable in keeping the public suspense building as day-by-day reports of the progress of the flight were beamed around the world.[20] Then, at the crest of the excitement, Earhart would land in triumph to capitalize on the book sales, speaking engagements, and endorsements arranged by Putnam.

The problem with any protracted delay was that the radio network consisted primarily of amateur enthusiasts who could not be expected to stay in readiness indefinitely. Even McMenamy and Pierson could not keep themselves available forever at their base station.

Nor, given the world's unstable political climate, could government overflight clearances be expected to hold up; nearly all had an expiration date, few carried a guarantee of renewal, and many had been only reluctantly issued in the first place, along with various restrictions and stipulations. As is still the case, many sovereign nations were simply not keen on the idea of having an American airplane cruise over their territories. The U.S. State Department had laboriously obtained the dozens of clearances necessary and would not be pleased to go through the whole tortuous process again.[21] Furthermore, there was nothing to keep a government from citing one of a variety of reasons for canceling an existing clearance if it chose. One perfectly valid reason, in fact, would have been concern that an incident like the Luke Field crash might occur within their jurisdiction.

Whether considering these matters or simply affirming her can-do personality, Earhart announced, almost as soon as the Electra stopped skidding, that she would reattempt the flight. Of course, this was precisely the right thing for the brave aviatrix and media darling to say immediately after emerging from a crash.

And she would mount another attempt, although the nature of her record attempt would be changed in ways that were kept hidden from public view. Now the U.S. government, which had been only indirectly participating in the planning and execution of the flight thus far, would become directly involved. In fact, military and political leaders would virtually take control of orchestrating every aspect of the operation from that point forward.[22]

We cannot know how Amelia Earhart felt about this turn of events, but it is unlikely that she had much choice. For one thing, the financial and logistical burdens had become too great for an individual enterprise.

A glance at only some of the raw costs of the flight will help fill out the picture. The Electra used aircraft fuel priced at 25 cents per gallon at the rate of fifty-three gallons an hour, giving a cost of $13.25 per hour. Flight time for the attempt was estimated at 250 hours, or a cost in fuel alone of $3,312.50. In addition, there were the costs of obtaining overflight clearances, food and lodging, salaries for personnel, oil, and the maintenance of the engine and the airframe (estimated to cost $10 per flight hour, or another $2,500). A rough ballpark estimate for the total cost of the attempt would be between $15,000 and $20,000. After the crash, however, another $30,000 would have to be invested to repair the Electra.[24] She herself acknowledged the financial situation in Last Flight by writing cryptically that, in order to keep going, she "mortgaged the future."[23] That mortgage included giving up control of her own flight and putting herself and her navigator in grave danger. Did she really consider all of the consequences? Our only clue is her breezy comment, "But without regrets, for what are futures for?"

CHAPTER FIVE

War

The time to worry is three months before a flight.
Decide then whether or not the goal is worth the
risks involved. If it is, stop worrying. To worry is
to add another hazard. It retards reactions, makes
one unfit. . . . Hamlet would have been a bad aviator. He worried too much.
   —Amelia Earhart, original foreword to *Last Flight*

To understand the opportunity that Amelia Earhart's flight presented to U.S. leaders, it is necessary to recall the military and
political realities of the late 1930s, particularly in regard to ominous Japanese activities in the Pacific.

Although that huge sea was as vast, desolate, and tranquil as it is today, its islands
and coastlines were in turmoil. These inti-
mations of the coming worldwide conflict
were legacies of the previous one, when
most of the Pacific islands were allocated as
the spoils of war to European nations or to
Japan. The U.S. also possessed a few of
them, most notably the Hawaiian chain,

and controlled other, apparently unimportant atolls such as the Line Islands, notwithstanding the previously mentioned uncertainty about legal jurisdiction.

Between the wars, most of these atolls had little peacetime value, except for the deposits of guano that could be sold as fertilizer. Even this enterprise had become commercially impractical by the late 1920s, and the trade was essentially abandoned. After that, the Line Islands lay undisturbed until Secretary Hull's secret memo and the subsequent construction on Howland.

American interests were also deeply involved in the Philippines, the former possessions that had only recently become semi-independent. Under a commonwealth agreement, the U.S. was pledged to defend them.

The problem was that Japan held most of Micronesia, the vast arc of widely scattered coral lagoons and tiny islands in the equatorial Western and Central Pacific. Colonized by Spain in the late eighteenth century, sold to Germany in the latter part of the nineteenth, the archipelago was snapped up by Japan as soon as she entered World War I on the side of the Allies. At war's end, the 1919 Versailles Treaty granted her continuing jurisdiction over all of Germany's Pacific islands north of the equator. The treaty specifically enjoined Japan from fortifying these so-called Mandated Islands or using them to base or train military personnel. Some of these islands, however, bore names with which a generation of Americans would become familiar in battles made bloody by the enemy's well-entrenched defense emplacements: Kwajalein, Saipan, Tarawa, Majuro.

Japan had closed the islands to outsiders by the mid-1930s. U.S. Naval Intelligence, relying upon sketchy reports from such diverse sources as missionaries, Korean intelligence agents, and employees of Pan American Airways, came to believe that the Japanese were illegally building military bases throughout Micronesia.

In addition to the Versailles agreement, international treaties in 1922 (Treaty of Washington, or Nine Power Treaty) and 1928 supposedly gave additional guarantees of peace in Asia and the Pacific Ocean region. The U.S. had either signed or supported each of these pacts but took no action when Japan violated the 1919 or 1922 treaties, the latter by conquering Manchuria in 1931. In truth, America was unable to mount any kind of credible response, even though it was now clear that Japan was on the march and granting ever more power to the militarists within its feudal government, whose watchword was "Expand or die."

They had come into power at the beginning of the decade, imbued with the belief that the national destiny was to control all of Southeast Asia and make use of the rich natural resources there in pursuit of world hegemony. They considered their emperor to be a divinity, themselves to be descendants of the Sun God. In support of a policy of expansion by conquest, they could draw upon a huge, modern military force, as well as a sizable population (eighty-nine million, as compared with Germany' seventy million and America's 127 million) and a large industrial base. After the invasion of Manchuria, Japan continued to fight more or less constantly in China. In 1937, she captured Peking, Tientsin, Shanghai, Nanking, and Hangchow, thus controlling most of lowland China.

Predictably, the island nation's budget tells the story best. Military expenditures amounted to 31 percent of the budget in 1931–32, then rose to 47 percent in 1936–37, before soaring to an astounding 70 percent in 1938.[1] In 1937, as Earhart began her first attempt to fly around the equator, the Japanese army consisted of twenty-four divisions and fifty-four air squadrons, including many veterans with considerable combat experience in China.

Another forty divisions were in the reserve forces.[2]

By contrast with this increasing military and political might, the U.S. airplanes based at Oahu were an accurate indication of the general state of America's military preparedness. Globally, the U.S. was a third-rate military power; in the Pacific, a distant second to Japan.

It has to be recalled, in addition, that the U.S. Army was tiny, a mere cadre maintained for the civilian volunteers expected to fight any future ground war. Total combat strength was equivalent to less than two divisions; the air corps that supported it was proportionately small. The U.S. Navy was far smaller than the Japanese fleet, its ships older, and its crews less well trained. These considerations loomed large in the high-level government decisions that would change the nature of Earhart's enterprise the second time around.

Why was the U.S. so weak in military strength? In the first place, the country had withdrawn wearily into isolationism in response to the butchery and betrayals of World War I; that sentiment remained strong. Such powerful senators as Gerald Nye of North Dakota, William E. Borah of Idaho, Hiram Johnson of California, Champ Clark of Minnesota, and Robert Taft of Ohio continued to inveigh against any involvement beyond the North American continent. In their view, supported by the majority of Americans, the great oceans provided adequate barriers, both physically and symbolically, to keep foreign enemies at bay.

The national disillusionment over the Great War sprang not just from the loss of American lives but also from the imposition of rationing of food and fuel, along with other basic necessities. Even more distasteful, to some, were the remarkable wartime limitations on personal freedom, including travel and written communication. Under President Woodrow Wilson, certain quasi-fascist tactics were employed to marshal public opinion in support of the war effort. For example, any civic, church, or school gathering might be spontaneously interrupted by an appearance of the so-called Seven-Minute Men, volunteer minions of the administration who were legally empowered to speak to any gathering for seven minutes about the Allied objectives in the war. Even in the late 1930s, such extraordinary departures from the norms of American life remained all too fresh in the collective national consciousness.

Most isolationists opposed any but a minimal military establishment; a substantial pacifist movement wanted all military forces disbanded. Ironically, in light of later historical developments, Franklin Roosevelt had come into office as an isolationist himself. He had even considered reducing military expenditures in the mid-1930s, in response to widespread public sentiment.

A second, equally important factor had prevented the U.S. from developing as a military power: lack of money. From its symbolic beginning with the Crash of 1929, the Great Depression had gripped the country, and indeed the world economy, throughout the decade of the 1930s. Considerable government funds were expended upon public works and in other ways to provide jobs and stimulate the economy. Military construction or related expenditures were not included in this effort, however, because of public opinion. After all, with the economy so severely depressed, tax revenues were sparse. According to the prevailing reasoning, what little money there was should be provided to the nation's impoverished citizenry.

Without funds to operate and maintain its ships, the navy stored some and scrapped others. The army trained with as few as one shot per year for the guns that required expensive ammunition. In such a climate, there was of course no money at all for research and development, much less for acquiring new weapons, aircraft, or other equipment. Furthermore, 1937 marked a downturn into a deep recession that threatened to swallow FDR's efforts to extricate the nation from its economic morass.

To oversimplify only slightly, then, it is fair to say that in 1937 America could not afford to prepare for war, even though it was clear that she would probably be forced to join the coming world conflict eventually, either in self-defense or in support of her allies abroad.

Yet, by failing to prepare beforehand, U.S. leaders placed European democracies and even their own population at considerable risk. The American people thus failed to see the war clouds gathering on the far horizon; the nation essentially chose to remain unprepared for war until well beyond its actual forced entry into the Pacific conflict on December 7, 1941.

On the other hand, the U.S. did have friends in the Pacific, including the several European nations, most notably Britain, that still held colonies in the region. Cosigners of the Versailles accord, they constituted the core of what would become the Allied powers in World War II. They had forces in place to protect their Pacific interests, and reserves to call upon at home. Taken together, the European military capability outweighed Japan's and could oppose her imperial aims against any Western nation's colonies. Japan had indeed been allowed to work her will in China, but China was not a *bona fide* member of the club.

In the event of a European war, however, these colonial forces would be called back to protect the home countries. As Adolf Hitler's Germany rearmed frantically and several nations became mired in the Spanish Civil War on one side or the other, that possibility was rapidly becoming a likelihood. In other words, in the late 1930s, astute observers could see that the stabilizing European military forces might well have to be withdrawn from the Pacific soon. Should that happen and Japan be allowed to build naval and air bases throughout the far-flung islands of Micronesia, she could turn the Pacific into a Japanese lake, at least for a while. How long it would then take the U.S. to match her warships in quality and quantity was an open question; experts disagreed. According to an estimate prepared by the War Department for FDR late in 1937, however, American forces could not reach an adequate level of strength for defense in the Pacific until 1943 to 1945. During that period, the U.S. would remain an inferior presence in the ocean that lapped at the shores of the West Coast and flowed into one entrance of the vital Panama Canal.

In short, events were rapidly proving the isolationists wrong. The Pacific and the Atlantic were no longer broad enough to provide adequate defense. Technological developments were shrinking the globe even as Japan's war machine was rapidly building island fortifications that would narrow the distance between its frontier and the U.S. mainland.

In the White House sat one of the shrewdest politicians ever to occupy it, a master of the art of the possible. That FDR did not share the credulity of his constituency has long been established. He was handicapped by the enormous limitations imposed upon him as head of a democratic republic, but he was a man accustomed to dealing with his handicaps with aplomb. Well understanding that the electorate determines what is possible, he would refuse time and time again throughout his four terms in office to take an action the country would not support, even when he and his advisers thought it advisable or necessary.

He had several times swayed public opinion, of course,

because he was an eloquent speaker and had learned to use his warm baritone effectively on the new means of mass communication, the radio. With his "fireside chats" he had been able to prevail over congressional opposition; conceivably, given sufficient proof that Japan was engaged in illegal and perfidious acts, he could go on the air and arouse the people of the United States from their torpor, despite their entrenched isolationist mood.

In the same vein, convincing proof could be brought before the World Court at the Hague. By the terms of Versailles and the U.S. Neutrality Act, America could not unilaterally intervene in the Pacific. The weak League of Nations could do little, either, having failed to stop Japan from invading Manchuria or Italy from taking Ethiopia. Besides, the U.S. was not a member of the League, and Japan had quit in 1933. A presentation at the Hague, however, might inspire enough international pressure to cause Japan at least to slow if not to halt her military buildup in Micronesia. The case would have to be solid; premature, unfounded, or peremptory accusations would only exacerbate an already volatile and steadily deteriorating diplomatic situation.

In other words, for two important and related reasons, it was clearly in the best interest of the United States to know the actual extent to which Japan was constructing military fortifications and facilities in the Mandated Islands, especially those nearest to Hawaii and the U.S. mainland. The Marshalls, located about two thousand miles southwest of Hawaii, were of greatest concern. The Roosevelt administration determined to find out what was going on; as suggested by the construction of the airfield on Howland Island, they also determined to put themselves in the position of obtaining proof that could be shown to the world.

Much more important in Roosevelt's view, intelligence

information from the Pacific (as well as from the other remote regions over which Earhart planned to fly) would be valuable for a variety of strategic purposes. Once the exact nature and scope of the Japanese threat was known, the appropriate response could be formulated.

FDR was further handicapped in achieving his goal because nothing existed that even remotely resembled the Central Intelligence Agency, the Defense Intelligence Agency, or any of the plethora of other government intelligence-gathering agencies that have come into being since the onset of World War II. The only government presence in the Pacific was the navy, which was not only limited in terms of available ships and manpower but also restricted in its activities by the terms of the Versailles Treaty.

Even so, some covert measures had been attempted, but all had failed. Among several Americans who tried to enter the mandates and gather information, Willard Price, a staff member of the National Geographic Society, narrowly escaped being captured by the Japanese while sailing near Truk atoll in the Marshalls.[3] He discovered later that two of his countrymen, both naval officers, had conducted an intelligence investigation in the same area in the mid- to late 1930s but had been discovered and executed. Although their bodies were never returned to the United States, the Japanese had given terse notification of their deaths through diplomatic channels. (Of course, as in the *Panay* gunboat incident, the U.S. was in no position to mount a credible protest; even less so, since the men were indeed caught in the very act of espionage.)

And there was the case of Marine Colonel Earl Ellis, who also tried to get information at Truk sometime in 1935–36, but never made it. He got only as far as Palau before he was caught. He, too, never returned.[4] These incidents undoubtedly made it clear to U.S. officials that any operation conducted in the South Central Pacific region, particularly near Truk, involved great risk.

The U.S. did have a kind of ersatz intelligence agency in the form of Pan American Airways, the only U.S. flag carrier operating internationally, as well as the largest airline in the world. In fact, the company's president, Juan Terry Trippe, openly referred to his airline as "the chosen instrument of the U.S. abroad."[5] The government subsidized Pan Am with contracts to carry the mail overseas. Even though the firm's bids for this business were routinely higher than those from other carriers, it was always awarded the contract. In return, Pan Am routinely performed certain delicate chores for the government, especially the gathering of information at outposts so remote the U.S. could not afford to maintain a presence there.

Unfortunately for FDR's problem in the Pacific, however, this relationship was all too widely known. Besides, none of Pan Am's regularly scheduled routes went anywhere near the Marshalls, and the company's big lumbering airplanes would be very easy to detect and shoot down if they were diverted for photo-intelligence purposes.

But the government was feeling increasing pressure to come up with some form of covert intelligence-gathering alternative fast. What the government knew or guessed was alarming enough. For example, it had become clear that Japan had set up phony civilian front organizations (e.g., Nanyo Kohatsu Kaisha, also known as the South Seas Development Corporation) to accomplish its military and political aims in the Mandates. Also, the meager intelligence sources in the Pacific agreed that a monstrous deep-water marine naval facility was being constructed at Truk.[6]

If the Roosevelt administration perceived these and other indications of expansionism to be untenable, dangerous, and, perhaps worst of all, frustrating, the Japanese

in their turn were consciously taking advantage of the ironies of the situation. They had factored in the military
weakness and isolationist mood of their only potential
rival in the Pacific region. They were actively employing a
double standard: denouncing the Versailles Treaty for
their own purposes, but using its provisions to keep the
U.S. out of the area.

The Japanese military establishment had noted well the
response to the 1931 invasion of Manchuria. They recalled the aftermath of the *Panay* incident. They concluded, in other words, that the Allied powers were unlikely, and probably unable, to challenge their advances.
Obviously, the U.S. would not violate international law
to intervene or directly confront them. Furthermore, they
could rely on the efficiency of their own measures to keep
the exact extent and intent of their activities secret. This
was decades before the U.S. or anyone else had the capability, considered routine today, to conduct a quantitative
covert survey of the nature and scope of military activities
anywhere in the world.

Into this situation, however, a Lockheed Electra, especially when highly modified and equipped with more powerful military-issue engines, might intrude with a reasonable chance of success. It could fly so high and so fast that,
in those days before operational radar, detection would
be unlikely. (Amelia Earhart, of course, had set her early
records as a high-altitude flyer.) Even if such an intruder
were detected and identified, however, the Japanese
would have no proof to offset a categorical denial from the
U.S.

Would the pilot be in mortal danger? Government officials must have reasoned that even the Japanese would
hesitate before shooting down Amelia Earhart, especially
since it could plausibly be claimed that she had simply
strayed off course.

As for pursuit, the Electra was fast and would start with a tremendous advantage in altitude. It could be assumed that short-range fighter planes would have to turn back before reaching Earhart's level, and that other aircraft would be too slow to catch up with her. These and many other, similarly reasonable assumptions might have been made, but in the event the Japanese were underestimated—an error the Americans would make again and again, before, during, and after World War II.

Whatever the reasoning at the highest levels of the U.S. government, it is now clear that the decision was made to take control of Earhart's world flight and keep that involvement strictly secret.

Thus simmered a recipe for intrigue.

DEPARTMENT OF STATE
WASHINGTON

February 13, 1935

My dear Mr. President:

Referring to your confidential memorandum of October 16, 1934, transmitting a copy of a letter from the Secretary of the Navy enclosing a memorandum from the Chief of Naval Operations concerning certain islands in the Pacific, including Jarvis, Howland and Baker Islands, it is believed that it would be desirable to place these islands by Executive Order under the administration of one of the Departments of the Government, possibly the Interior Department.

Each of these three islands has been included in the list of bonded guano islands published by the Treasury Department, and the Secretary of State issued on August 7, 1860, a guano certificate for Howland to the United States Guano

The President,

The White House.

a

1. This memorandum (a) to the president from Secretary of State Cordell Hull and President Roosevelt's reply (b) were the first indication of U.S. government efforts to establish a presence in the Central Pacific. *Franklin D. Roosevelt Library, Hyde Park, N.Y.*

Guano Company, and on March

for both Jarvis and Baker to the American Guano Company.
The courts of this country have held that the effect of
such certificate is to place the island under the jurisdiction of the United States as appurtenant thereto.

Prior to the issuance of these certificates, possession in the name of the United States was formally taken
to both Jarvis and Baker Islands by Captain Davis on the
United States Sloop of War ST. MARY'S on August 16 and 24,
respectively, 1857. While a similar action does not appear
to have been taken with respect to Howland Island, the latter island was, it seems, discovered by an American citizen,
Captain George E. Netcher, on September 9, 1842. It is
possible that the other two islands were not discovered by
Americans.

Between March 25 and April 1, 1935, the ITASCA landed
several Americans (Hawaiians) on each of the three islands,
and they have been continuously occupied since then. On
several occasions other men have been sent out to replace
those on each island. In addition, it is understood that
an American guano company has been operating on the islands
since some time last summer or the early fall. Prior thereto, the islands had not been operated for guano for many
years.

Many

a

-3-

Many years subsequent to

can jurisdiction over the islands, various British pub-
lications have from time to time, listed one or another,
or all of these islands as under British jurisdiction,
and it has been stated that they were leased to British
companies in the latter years of the last, or the early
years of the present century. It is also stated that
Jarvis was annexed to Great Britain on June 3, 1889, by
Commander Nichols of H.M.S. CORMORANT. This was some
thirty-two years after possession of the island had been
formally taken for the United States by Captain Davis of
the United States Sloop of War ST. MARY'S. I am unaware,
however, of any formal action on the part of the British
Government seeking definitely to place these islands by
name under British jurisdiction, and there has been no
correspondence between the two Governments in the matter.

Whatever, if any, occupation of the islands there
may have been by British companies, it appears that at
the time of the ITASCA's arrival last spring, all three
of them had been abandoned for many years. The report
of the expedition of the U.S.S. TANAGER and WHIPPOORWILL
in 1924 states that when the islands were visited at
that time, they were then all uninhabited and showed no
signs of current exploitation of any kind.

Wide

a

Wide publicity has been given in the United States last spring with respect to the islands, but no representations in regard thereto have been made by the British Government. In view of all the circumstances in the case I think that an Executive Order could be issued placing these islands under the jurisdiction of one of the Departments of the Government without first communicating in the matter with the British Government.

It is interesting to note in this connection, that a number of guano islands in the Pacific contained in the Treasury's list of bonded guano islands, have been formally placed by Orders in Council under British jurisdiction without the British Government communicating beforehand with this Government to ascertain its views.

Faithfully yours,

Cordell Hull

a

THE WHITE HOUSE
WASHINGTON

February 19, 1936.

MEMORANDUM FOR

THE SECRETARY OF STATE

I entirely approve an
Executive Order placing these
Islands under the Interior Department. Will you speak with the
Secretary of the Interior about
it and have the necessary Order
prepared?

F. D. R.

Let. from the Secy. of State 2/18/36 - copy retained.

x48

b

NAVY DEPARTMENT
OFFICE OF CHIEF OF NAVAL OPERATIONS
WASHINGTON

16 November, 1936

Memorandum:

For: The Chief of Naval Operations.

The attached letter was handed me this morning,
together with the information that the President
hoped the Navy would do what they could to cooperate
with Miss Amelia Earhart in her proposed flight and
that in this connection, contact should be made with
her husband, Mr. Putnam.

Paul Bastedo.

NOV 18 1936

2. As early as November 1936, President Roosevelt directed the U.S. Navy to "cooperate" with Amelia Earhart in her proposed around-the-world flight. *Navy and Old Military Branch, National Archives, Washington, D.C.*

TELEGRAM

The White House
Washington

15WUC 22 GOVT   8:12 p.m.

Oakland, California, 4:50 p.m. March 17, 1937.

The White House;

    Miss Earhart departed from Oakland Airport for Honolulu at four thirty-two Pacific time this date on her around-the-world flight.

                    W. T. Miller.

3. William T. Miller, a naval intelligence officer acting as an official, sometimes with the Department of the Interior, Department of Island Territories and Possession, and at other times attached to the Department of Commerce, Bureau of Air Commerce, actually worked directly for the Roosevelt White House, keeping the upper-echelon personnel there informed up to the minute on Amelia Earhart's activities. *Obtained from declassified U.S. Naval Intelligence files under the Freedom of Information Act.*

4. Amelia Earhart with Walter B. McMenamy in front of her Lockheed Electra during a press briefing on her world-flight plans. McMenamy was retained as a technical adviser on matters relating to the installation of radios aboard the Electra, and was in charge of establishing a worldwide radio communications network to monitor and report the progress of the flight. *Author's photo collection*

5. *Left to right,* George Palmer Putnam; Amelia Earhart; Harry Manning, navigator-designate for the first world-flight attempt; and mechanic Bo McKneely. Los Angeles, February 24, 1937. *National Archives, Washington, D.C.*

6. Disaster struck as Amelia Earhart, accompanied by crew members Harry Manning and Fred Noonan, crashed while attempting to take off from Luke Field, Hawaii, an Army Air Corps airfield, on the morning of March 20, 1937. This flight, from Honolulu to Howland Island, was to be the second leg of the first world-flight attempt. The Electra, severely damaged, was crated by the army, and shipped back to Los Angeles via steamship, arriving there at the end of March. *Pan Pacific Press Bureau*

CHAPTER SIX

Reverse Course

I recall that I was directed to cut two 16–18 inch diameter holes for the cameras, which were to be mounted in the lower aft fuselage bay and would be electrically operated. . . .
—Robert T. Elliott, Lockheed technician, interview with author

All documents, reports, memoranda, and correspondence between the U.S. Navy/ Roosevelt administration and either or both of the Putnams were classified "secret." They were not seen by nonparticipants for the next fifty years.

The earlier signs of official involvement—the proposed air-to-air refueling mission, the substitution of the Howland Island scheme, the participation of Navy Captain Harry Manning as a navigator— were only the tip of the iceberg, even before the Luke Field crash.

At government expense, all of the maps for Earhart's flight had been prepared by

Captain Clarence Williams, a cartographer in the Office of Cartographic Services in the Naval Bureau of Navigation.[1] The superintendent of airways for the Commerce Department, William T. Miller, had been assigned by Commerce Secretary Daniel Roper to serve as the administration's liaison with Earhart during her planning of the flight.[2]

During her preparations, she was given permission to use the facilities at March Army Air Base, near Riverside, California. Normally, such military installations are strictly off limits to private activities. In fact, then as now, laws and regulations prohibited the use of public property for the sole benefit of any private individual. Aside from matters of security, the military wanted to avoid possible liability in incidents like the crash in Oahu. Finally, the financially strapped military could not afford to fuel its own aircraft, much less provide fuel for Amelia Earhart. But photographs show the Electra, surrounded by armed military police, being refueled at the base. (See illus. 7.) Of course, Luke Field, too, was an Army Air Corps facility.

None of these things would have been allowed without orders to the military from the highest possible level. Besides, in this era before the creation of a Department of Defense, the army and the navy were virtually independent and rival kingdoms. Only the president of the United States, the constitutional commander-in-chief, could have forced the two services to cooperate in supporting the Earhart flight.

Publicly, the government continues to claim that Amelia Earhart was engaged in a strictly civilian flight, but a photograph proves just the opposite. (See illus. 8.) According to Earhart's aide and secretary, Margo de Carrie, a number of very senior military officers visited the Putnams' California home while flight preparations were under way. She also recalled that a significant turning point in the involvement of the military occurred after Earhart met with General Henry H. "Hap" Arnold and General Oscar Westover (then head of the U.S. Army Air Forces) at March Army Air Base. At one of these two meetings, or at some other point, officials were able to convince Amelia to accept a direct commission into the U.S. military, as major, USAAF. In the photograph, she is being sworn into service. (The precise date and location of the picture are not known.)

FDR's proclivity for secrecy, which has only been clearly revealed in the years since his death, allowed for little written record of his discussions, directives, aims, or motives in regard to the Earhart flight. What evidence does exist, therefore, is of major significance. In addition to the original order to the chief of naval operations to "assist in any way we can," there still exists the detailed exchange of memoranda between the president, Secretary of State Cordell Hull, and Rex Martin, assistant director of air commerce for air navigation, regarding the construction of the airfield on Howland Island, supposedly for Earhart's use alone.[3]

But he took pains to distance himself from the project, and with good reason. The possibility of American involvement in foreign conflicts had been an issue in the 1936 campaign, and Roosevelt remained vulnerable. He had been accused at various times of being a "warmonger," because he advocated a greater degree of military preparedness. Congressional adversaries sparred with him over the dilemma of how to embargo belligerent nations but at the same time lend assistance to America's allies overseas. At this particular time, in this particular political atmosphere, Roosevelt did not want to be caught initiating actions to claim and fortify Pacific Islands that lay halfway across the globe, right on the threshold of Japan's sphere of influence.

Yet he wanted to protect the Line Islands in particular, and prepare them for use by U.S. forces, if and when the need arose. His administration's involvement in the Howland Island project and its military potential were therefore soft-pedaled by bureaucratic obfuscation. The aviation facilities were to be developed by the Commerce Department's Bureau of Air Commerce. For administrative purposes, the Line Islands were transferred from the control of the Navy Department to the obscure Division of Islands and Territories in the Department of the Interior.

In that vein, the construction of the Howland Island airfield was at one time overseen by Robert L. Campbell, an airport inspector for the Department of Commerce's Bureau of Airports. But the participation of others seems less innocuous. For example, there was the mysterious William T. Miller. Under the guise of a harmless civil servant, he functioned as a sort of all-round handyman for secret projects. In this instance, he took four American "colonists" to the island to serve as the Commerce Department's custodians.

Equally at home with subterfuge was Rex Martin, who, besides serving as assistant director of air commerce for air navigation, was also an aide to Air Commerce Bureau Director Eugene Vidal. According to White House documents classified until recently, Martin devised an elaborate cover story, including the recommendation that a post-office official lie to the press if necessary. The details of his scheme were set down in a memorandum to the president dated April 8, 1935, and marked "confidential":

To date there is no public knowledge concerning the proposed plan for sovereignty over the islands of Jarvis, Howland and Baker. Should anything become public in connection therewith, it is advisable that all concerned make the same public statements.

Newspaper correspondents will obviously demand an explanation from the Department of Commerce as to why these islands are being colonized. To say that it is for the purpose of installing air navigation facilities to aid ocean flying would obviously require a tentative projection of an airmail service in the Pacific. The Second Assistant Postmaster General [Harlee Branch], in charge of Air Mail Service, has informally agreed to make such an announcement at the proper time. To aid in the appearance of fact, the attached charts [have been prepared], and will remain confidential until such time as a public explanation is demanded.

The claim for sovereignty by the United States is being handled by the State Department, and no agency other than the State Department will discuss this phase without prior consultation with the State Department. . . .[4]

Clearly, no such airmail flights were ever contemplated. By the way, history would soon vindicate the Roosevelt administration's preoccupation with tiny Howland. It is perhaps appropriate to leap forward briefly and consider what would happen later. In the first place, the very existence of the island helped determine the route the Japanese took to attack Pearl Harbor. Their closest bases to Hawaii were those they had begun building in the Marshall Islands in 1936, but sea-lanes from there could be observed from Howland, thus denying the attackers the advantage of surprise. At least partly for this reason, the fleet would sail directly from Japan to Hawaii, more than half again the distance from the Marshalls to the target. Although the lengthier trip exposed the ships to accidental discovery for a longer period of time, the notoriously bad weather in that part of the ocean was likely to provide cover. More important, no island base upon which the U.S. had reconnaissance planes lay along this route.

Immediately after Pearl Harbor, Howland Island was the second U.S. territory to be attacked. A part of the fleet had headed south to the Marshalls for fuel and other supplies; en route, the Japanese carrier-based planes blasted the Howland airfield into cratered uselessness. They also bombed and strafed every vehicle and building, effectively destroying all equipment and housing on the island. Two of the American "colonists" were killed in the onslaught; the others would not be evacuated by the U.S. Navy until January 15, 1942. After the attack, neither side would use the island. The bomb damage has never been repaired, and birds have taken the place over in the peaceful years since.[5]

Earhart's original route, which had necessitated her husband's request for navy help in air-to-air refueling, would have passed far north of Howland. It would have also involved a payment of $1,000 to the navy for services rendered. Once the decision was made to switch to Howland Island, however, there was no mention, official or otherwise, of Earhart's paying for or provisioning the airfield that was purportedly being built only for her flight. On the contrary, FDR ordered a $3,000 appropriation to the Works Progress Administration for building and provisioning the new airfield. Military installations and supplies were suddenly made available to the Earhart project at no cost.

When was the deal struck? We can certainly see that Amelia's role in the government's schemes was passive until the accident at Luke Field; sometime before she began her second attempt at the world record, she became an active participant in espionage—or, in a word, a spy.

Certain facts do stand out boldly in the period between the two attempts. At first, the broken Electra was dismantled and crated by Army Air Corps personnel for shipment to the Lockheed plant in Burbank, California. Company officials announced that it would be repaired. The Putnams apparently intended to continue their previous course, in every sense of the word. In fact, however, their plans had come to a dead stop for lack of funds.[6]

Then to the Earharts' home in the Toluca Lake section of Hollywood came an emissary directly from the Oval Office, the so-called adviser to presidents and wealthy financier Bernard B. Baruch. According to Margo de Carrie, who was present during portions of three separate meetings between Baruch and the Putnams over a period in late March and early April, the presidential intimate talked with Amelia about volunteering for an intelligence mission that would be assisted and underwritten by the military.[7] He offered a powerful inducement: the wherewithal to continue the flight.

Not long afterward, de Carrie, who had handled the many clerical details of the first attempt, began to notice something strange this time around. No bills came in, not for aircraft expenses, repairs, fuel, hangar storage, or anything else. She would also recall later, as would Walter McMenamy, that the shadowy William T. Miller took up residence in the Putnams' house shortly after Baruch's last visit, and involved himself in the details of planning the second attempt.[8]

These included yet another dramatic change: the public soon learned that the flight would be made this time in the opposite direction, from west to east. Amelia offered the explanation, implausible but accepted, that the switch was necessitated by a seasonal change in wind patterns.[9] In fact, little seasonal change of any sort occurs in weather along the equator, and no change at all in wind direction. The prevailing wind is always from east to west, the opposite direction from the wind in the Northern and Southern hemispheres. That was the reason she had chosen to fly from east to west in the first place. Now she would be bucking the prevailing wind, which made no sense at all. Even allowing for the general public's credulity or ignorance, it seems unbelievable that other aviators, such as the Pan Am Pacific Clipper pilots, did not question the change. Publicly, at least, none ever did.

What made no sense for an aviator, however, would make a lot of sense for a spy taking aerial photographs of Japanese installations in the Marshall Islands. Going east to west, Earhart would have landed immediately afterward at Lae, New Guinea, where many civilians would have crowded round to greet her. Lae was foreign territory, and any one of a thousand things could go wrong, not the least of which would be the discovery of the bulky camera. Air New Guinea personnel were familiar with the Lockheed Electra and would notice anything unusual about the specifications of the plane. If they discovered the camera, which would suggest that the flight was not quite the innocent civilian-daredevil stunt it was supposed to be, their government might well confiscate the film. At the very least, such a discovery would jeopardize further attempts to make reconnaissance flights over the Mandates.

Even if she was not unmasked in Lae, she would have had to fly two-thirds of the way around the world with the equipment and film still on board, unless risky arrangements were made to intercept her in New Guinea or Australia. After that, San Juan, Puerto Rico, was the first U.S. territory she would touch, then Miami, Florida, after that. In both places, her every action was likely to be exposed to full view.

By going from west to east, however, Earhart could land on isolated, remote, U.S.-government-controlled Howland immediately after passing above the Marshalls. There the film could be retrieved and the cameras removed in absolute secrecy before she flew on to what would no doubt be a tumultuous welcome in Hawaii.

But there was another difficulty, in addition to the actual direction of the prevailing wind, brought on by the decision to fly from west to east. Although it has been suggested that the odds of finding her destination were better if she flew from Howland to Lae, that is ludicrous on its face. As Amelia herself put it in planning her original attempt, "It's easier to hit a continent than an island."[10] New Guinea is, of course, an island, but a huge island, many times larger than tiny Howland.

There was another positive reason, aside from concealing photographic equipment, for flying from west to east. As Earhart took off from Lae, she would be tracked by the *Itasca*, which would be standing by at Howland.

For about a year, the Coast Guard cutter had been doing duty in relation to the establishment of U.S. facilities on the Line Islands as well as the islands in the Canton-Enderbury group. It had been designated to participate as a radio ship in Earhart's first attempt. Since the accident, it had joined the USS *William J. Duane* in shuttling materials and personnel between the various islands of the Central Pacific that were the focus of secret U.S. government activity.

Now the *Itasca* was outfitted with the navy's new top-secret direction-finding [DF] equipment, as well as ordinary low- and high-frequency communications radios. The classified equipment was brought aboard in Honolulu by a U.S. intelligence officer, Captain, later Admiral, Richard Blackburn Black. In theory, the navy would be able to track the Earhart plane accurately by means of her radio transmissions, even if she spoke for only thirty seconds or simply held down the mike button. Locating her radio signal, the radiomen could either give her a course heading directly to the ship or steer her toward another objective by giving her headings based upon the DF bearings. Or she could use her DF equipment on board the Electra to locate a signal from the ship and aim toward it.

Considering all of the diverse factors discussed above, therefore, the decision to change direction, thus flying from Lae to Howland, was eminently sensible, from the point of view of a government wanting to manage a clandestine operation and get away with it.

In addition to the choice of direction for the flight, other profound changes clearly indicate the true nature of Earhart's second attempt. Not least was a dramatic turnabout in the mood of the undertaking. According to McMenamy, among others, a ponderous atmosphere of grim urgency suddenly descended.[11] Gone entirely was the lighthearted spirit of the first attempt, which Amelia had characterized as "just for fun." There would be no more amusing antics, like Paul Mantz hitching a ride at the last minute to see his fiancée. Amelia's personal challenge had become something else: a mission.

McMenamy recalls the contrast as palpable. On March 4, only two weeks before the first attempt, Amelia had written him in a chipper, optimistic mood:

> It is pleasant that you are helping me with radio communication matters on my forth-coming flight. I so much appreciated your work and cooperation on the Pacific hop in 1935. You were in contact with me from the time I left Honolulu until I came down to Oakland. Let's hope we have as good luck this time.[12]

After the very bad luck at Luke Field, Amelia returned to Long Beach aboard the SS *Mololo*. McMenamy and his colleague Karl Pierson went to meet the ship, hoping to assure Earhart that they still supported her and would continue to give assistance. To McMenamy's shock, she was escorted down the gangplank by a phalanx of navy personnel and rushed past him and Pierson to a waiting navy automobile. Though he had of course been working within the inner circle of her advisers, now he could make only brief eye contact with her. She recognized him with a wan smile but brushed past without a word. Years later, he still remembered his astonishment that she seemed so uncharacteristically subdued and downcast.

Amelia Earhart would never again speak to Walter McMenamy.[13]

Meanwhile, unknown to the public, the question of repairs to the Electra had been mooted in a very expensive way.

"By the time she returned [to the mainland], there was a new airplane ready for her," said Robert T. Elliott, an airframe technician at Lockheed at the time. "This one was a Model 12."[14]

Outwardly similar to the Model 10E, the new plane actually incorporated two highly significant technical differences. Without them, the Earhart flight could have ended more or less as traditional historians have believed. But because of these important new factors, which have not been revealed until now, we can consider the traditional version entirely discredited. It is important to look at them closely.

Controversy has surrounded the question of exactly which model of Lockheed Electra aircraft Amelia Earhart was flying when she disappeared. Part of the explanation lies in the manner in which aircraft were built at the Lockheed Aircraft Company factory in the 1930s.

Many aircraft were under construction at once, in varying stages of completion, but the aircraft types were limited to two, the Model 10 Electra, and the Model 12 Electra Junior. There was little outward difference; the Model 12 Electra Junior was slightly smaller than the Model 10 Electra. It was also lighter and faster. In any event, as the airplanes were assembled at the LAC factory, the similarities between the designs far outnumbered the differences, and the engineers and technicians could—and did—virtually hand-build the planes. No two were alike. Each was, in effect, a hybrid, designed and built with its particular customer and mission in mind.

The airplane Amelia flew around the world was a hybrid in many important ways. It had the size, outward appearance, and higher gross weight of the Model 10, along with the larger 550-horsepower Pratt & Whitney Wasp Senior engines; yet it was fitted with the more advanced constant-speed propellers of the Model 12. It also was capable of the Model 12's speed—as high as 240 miles per hour in level cruise flight. The plane was undoubtedly constructed using many Model 12 components, as R. T. Elliott has stated, and many others have suggested.

These factors, in addition to some relatively slight modifications to the fuselage, gave the aircraft a larger effective payload than the original 10E. In other words, it could carry more simply because the difference between its basic weight and its maximum allowable weight was greater. (Today the difference would be expressed in a technically exact power-to-weight ratio.) In sum, Earhart would have an aircraft that could climb much higher and fly much faster than her original Electra; to be specific, it was capable of cruising at speeds up to 220 miles per hour, as compared with 140. Obviously, the secret changes meant that Amelia could zip off an announced course and then return to her route without the public, at least, being any the wiser. Her new altitude capacity, so crucial to any espionage overflight, was also concealed.

To enhance the deception that she was still flying the original, restored airplane, the identification number (NR16020) was painted on the plane's wings and tail. Firming up the cover story, virtually every one of the administration's internal communications involved secrecy, along with diversion of press and public attention at every turn.

One participant in the fuselage modification was Lockheed airframe technician Robert T. Elliott, an eleven-year veteran of Lockheed Aircraft Company, and a faculty member at Mount San Antonio College in California for thirty-two years. His recollection gets to the heart of the matter, revealing the government's primary aim in supervising the work on the airplane:

> There was an Electra airplane off the regular line.
>
> I recall that I was called off my regular duties several times to go to the experimental area. I was then directed to cut two 16–18 inch diameter holes to be used for the cameras [Fairchild aerial-survey cameras, as documentation found later would show; see p. 174], which were to be mounted in the lower aft fuselage bay and would be electrically operated. There was a lot of modification required for this equipment. This was all done in the old Lockheed plant in Burbank, California. That bit about repairing her crashed Model 10 was just a ruse.

Once the secret modifications were completed, Amelia began intensive training with the new airplane, as necessitated by its added power and higher gross weight. To his dismay, Mantz was replaced as trainer and technical adviser by Lockheed's Clarence L. (Kelly) Johnson. The lat-

ter, a major player in the early development of the Skunk-
works,—as Lockheed's top-secret experimental aircraft
shop was called—was much better qualified for the task,
however.

Significantly, because it went against her usual practice,
Amelia made little or no effort to publicize herself during
the period between March 17 and the end of May, when
preparations for the flight were again under way. Maintaining a low profile, she gave few newspaper or radio
interviews, in contrast to her usual practice of being in the
news on a more or less daily basis.

Nor did she set down the details of her planning. In *Last
Flight*, she merely noted that she "managed to spend some
time with friends," referring to Jackie Cochran and her
husband, who had a ranch in secluded Indio, California.
Such visits were of necessity rare, though, for she was
busy, according to the record, practicing with the Electra
under "high load flight conditions."[15]

She was also waging a battle with Putnam about the
hiring of Fred Noonan as navigator.[16] Ever concerned
about the optimal apportionment of glory, her husband
had long argued in favor of a solo world flight, at least for
part of the route. He fretted that a navigator would inevitably have to share some of the publicity. Noonan was
particularly unsuitable in this regard, because he still carried some small cachet as a formerly renowned Pan Am
navigator. (The government's position on this matter is
not known, although we can speculate that officials would
probably have preferred that she have a navigator along
on such a sensitive expedition.)

But Amelia, as the world's most experienced long-
distance pilot and record-setter, knew that a globe-
circling flight over the longest possible route in a twin-
engine plane was too much for one person alone.
Understandably, she wanted a competent, experienced

navigator flying with her. Captain Harry Manning was considered as an alternative to Noonan, but he had returned to command of his ship, the USS *United States*. Besides, whether out of compassion for someone who wanted to make a comeback or out of respect for his ability, Amelia firmly supported the choice of Noonan. She won the struggle with her husband: she and Fred Noonan would make the flight together all the way.[17]

Another familiar member of her team, however, would be unceremoniously cast aside for this second attempt, even though he had already devoted a great deal of time, effort, contacts, and equipment to the project at Amelia's personal request. In an interview in 1980, he explained what happened:

> After she crashed in the Hawaiian Islands . . . the navy and Coast Guard completely took over the flight. Amelia herself made no decisions anymore, and we had no contact with her. I used to see her at least a couple of times a week, but after the Luke Field episode, I never spoke with Amelia again. U.S. [FBI] agents called us to a meeting at a Los Angeles restaurant, and swore Karl [Pierson] and I to secrecy about the flight and the radio signals we received up on the [Beacon] hill.[18]

McMenamy was told that all of Amelia's radio messages to be released to the press would be channeled through the Beacon Hill station. According to the FBI agents who spoke with him and Pierson, some of the messages would be deliberately false, because the media were not to know her whereabouts at all times. (The *Los Angeles Times* had bought first rights to the information from Putnam, and that agreement could not be abrogated now.)

> The only reason we remained involved at all was because they needed our technical expertise and our equipment.

They knew we'd be able to monitor Amelia's signals anyway, which we did. They didn't like it. But they wanted to keep us under their control. They appealed to our patriotic sense, and of course that worked.[19]

McMenamy went on to explain that he had felt obligated to honor his secrecy pledge in the years after Earhart's disappearance. When he decided at last to reveal his story, he requested an official release from his vow. His request was granted by U.S. Attorney General Benjamin Civiletti in a formal letter in 1979.

Amelia's unsuccessful suitor Lloyd Royer, the engineer who worked at Lockheed during 1935–36, also knew something of the story. In an interview shortly after the fortieth anniversary of Earhart's disappearance, he explained that he had "worked on her first Electra, but the final flight was made in a different plane."[20]

CHAPTER SEVEN

The Attempt

... always we found my usual calling cards, fifty-gallon drums of gasoline, each with my name printed large upon it in white or red lettering. The exact quantity of fuel, all as arranged months before ...

—Amelia Earhart, *Last Flight*

On May 18, all preparations complete, Lockheed turned the Electra over to Amelia at Burbank.

Now, with everything in place, there was no longer any need for reticence, at least in the PR mind of George Palmer Putnam. Besides, nothing would have seemed more natural (and thus perfect for the aims of the government) than for the publicity bandwagon to roll out full-speed. On the 20th, with Mantz at her side, Amelia flew the craft north to Oakland. There, as part of one of her husband's money-making schemes, Amelia and Mantz, along with the Putnams' longtime friend Elmer H. Dimity, loaded sixty-five hundred presold

first-day-of-issue philatelic covers into the Electra. Earhart
and Mantz then flew back to Burbank. He left for St.
Louis, where he was to appear in an aerobatic competition
the following day. Supposedly, Amelia intended to spend
several more days making final preparations before heading for Miami to start the world flight. To Mantz's astonishment, however, she made an unannounced departure
eastward the very next day, taking along Putnam, Noonan, and her principal mechanic, "Bo" McKneely. Thus
Mantz joined the swelling ranks of civilian aides, advisers,
and volunteers summarily ejected from the Earhart inner
circle. All had been replaced by representatives of the administration, the navy, the army, and the Department of
Commerce.[1]

The leg from Oakland to Miami was intended partly as
a shakedown flight: if trouble developed, it would be easy
enough to return to Burbank for factory repairs. For that
reason, prudence might have dictated keeping a low profile; no one involved wanted to risk the kind of embarrassment that would be caused by mechanical failure at this
juncture.

On the other hand, Lockheed had exhaustively tested
the aircraft, and it had performed without a hitch in many
hours of flying, including the round trip to Oakland, so
trouble was really not expected. A more likely reason for
the secret departure was the fear that nosy reporters pok-
ing around the plane before a well-publicized takeoff, as
was typical, would discover the special equipment, or
even recognize that this Electra was not the one they had
seen and photographed only two months before.

Perhaps this worry was unnecessary. Not only did the
press and public not make anything of the abrupt departure from Burbank; apparently, no one thought there was
anything unusual in what happened next. The aircraft that
had just spent months in Lockheed's factory facilities was

now detained for a week in Pan Am's maintenance hangar. The reason, according to U.S. Navy information, was that Pan Am was responsible for installing the secret new long-range low-frequency DF equipment needed for communication with the secret new installation aboard the *Itasca*. After all, it was at least partly to test the DF outfit for the military that the Electra had been provided to Earhart in the first place.

The secret refitting has led to one specific misunderstanding. At the last minute, nearly five hundred pounds of standard direction-finding radio and its cumbersome, 250-foot-long, trailing antenna equipment was removed from the plane. The reason given publicly was to save weight. Some theorists, unaware of the secret DF installation, have argued that the removal of the standard equipment made it impossible for Earhart and Noonan to find Howland and may have cost them their lives.

As we know now, however, the new, more sophisticated DF system, similar to today's automatic direction-finder (ADF), could point directly to a radio station over long distances, giving Earhart and Noonan more, not less, direction-finding capability for their flight. It employed a much more powerful and efficient antenna than the older system's, mounted atop the fuselage, with wires leading back to the vertical tail fins. Also, the previous equipment included a long, trailing wire weighing over four hundred pounds, a burden that would probably have made takeoff from Lae impossible, since so much fuel needed to be loaded aboard for that leg of the trip.

Over the years, much conjecture has centered on the decision to leave behind the radio-direction-finder trailing antenna. Some have even suggested that the absence of the device caused or contributed to the flyers' disappearance. This was not the case, for the simple reason that the newer ADF radio with which the Electra was equipped did not

require the cumbersome, heavy, trailing-wire type of antenna, but relied instead upon a much smaller, state-of-
the-art wire aerial that was attached to the structure of the
aircraft.

Some theorists have also postulated that lack of the
proper antenna, or the very few radio transmissions Amelia made during the final flight, or improper operation of
the radios, either separately or in combination, resulted in
Earhart's not being able to find Howland Island. This, too,
is incorrect, based on faulty assumptions.

To begin with, it is evident from the few short radio
transmissions Amelia made that she was not attempting to
obtain a direction-finder "steer" from the *Itasca* radio operator. At the same time, if she were attempting to
"home"—i.e., steer toward the *Itasca*'s radio signals,
guided by the ADF radio receiver aboard the Electra—she
could easily have done so, given the surfeit of signals
broadcast by the *Itasca*'s radiomen. The Electra was
equipped with the best ADF set then made, and Amelia's
ADF needle could have locked onto the *Itasca* signals
from as far away as two hundred miles. It is clear she was
not attempting to use the device for that purpose.

(By the way, given the developing technology of the
day, it is no exaggeration to compare the preparations for
Amelia Earhart's attempt to the difficulty and complexity
of the launch of a NASA space shuttle today. Senator
John Glenn, first U.S. astronaut to orbit in space, has said
that the dangers Amelia faced most certainly equaled
those of his flight.)

After the week's delay, Earhart was ready to begin.
Now, for the first time, press releases began to be released
on a regular basis from Beacon Hill. The navy made certain that the public knew that these carefully controlled
broadcasts were "official," and took pains to declare that
any others would be hoaxes. The doctored "exclusives"

bought by the *Los Angeles Times* were sent out on the wire services and picked up by newspapers and radio stations around the world.

The progress of the flight can be followed in summaries of these reports, but only with enlightened skepticism, since we now know that the navy's heavy hand lay upon the story they seem to tell.

June 1. Without announcing their intention publicly or otherwise alerting the press, Earhart and Noonan left Miami at 5:47 A.M. (EST) for San Juan, Puerto Rico. In *Last Flight*, Amelia described the dawn as "brilliant" and wrote that she stayed tuned to Miami's WQAM for continuing reports on the weather that lay ahead. Pan Am had arranged for the commercial station to broadcast this information. In other words, she did not rely upon McMenamy's radio network, which had ostensibly been set up in large part to relay weather reports. Every half-hour, at fifteen and forty-five minutes past the hour, she sent position reports back to WQAM.

As this momentous challenge began at last, Earhart demonstrated her characteristic facility with language in describing the world that unfolded beneath her:

> At six thirty we sighted the great reef of the Bahama banks. At about seven o'clock, Andros Island stretched out as a vivid green rug before our eyes. The fringe of that rug was formed by the varicolored tendrils of the sea reaching finger-like into the islands, some resembling vivid green snakes wriggling in a maritime Garden of Eden.
>
> The beauties of these tropic seas viewed from the air were in sharp contrast to the leaden dullness of the North Atlantic and far reaches of the Pacific Ocean, as I have seen them from aloft.[2]

The pair landed in San Juan early in the afternoon after a flight of eight hours, seventeen minutes. Amelia lunched with Mrs. Thomas Rodenbaugh, wife of the manager of the local Pan Am facility. Then, declining the hospitality of Acting Governor Menéndez Ramos, she and Noonan stayed overnight at the plantation home of Amelia's pilot friend Clara Livingston. Summing up this first segment of the flight in her journal, Earhart felt compelled for some reason to explain why she had chosen to "just slip away" without a word to press or public.

> The fact is that the career of one who indulges in any flight off the beaten path is often complicated. . . . So I am hoping the pros and cons of the whole undertaking can wait until it is finally over. If I am successful, the merits and demerits can be threshed out then. If not, someone else will do what I have attempted and I will pass the problem on to him—or her.[3]

June 2. Earhart's original plan to go next to Paramaribo, the capital of Dutch Guiana, a flight of about twelve hundred miles, had to be scuttled, for two reasons. Runway construction at the San Juan airport made it inadvisable to take off fully loaded with fuel, and there was a lack of possible intermediate stops along the route for use in case of trouble. It was decided to break up the trip and make a stopover in Caripito, Venezuela.

The pair arrived there, after a four-hour flight, at 10:18 A.M. (EST). Amelia recorded in her notes that Caripito had a very good field, complete with paved runways and a modern, well-equipped hangar jointly owned by Pan Am and the Standard Oil Company.[4]

They were greeted by Don Andrés Rolando, president of the state of Monagas, and its secretary general, Don Ramiro Rendiles. Overnight accommodations were provided courtesy of Henry E. Linam, general manager of the Standard Oil Company of Venezuela. After an evening Earhart described as pleasant, she and Noonan got under

way in the early hours of the following morning. Dodging
dense clouds and rain showers, they now pressed gamely
on toward Paramaribo.

June 3. Scribbled high above the towering cumulus
clouds, Amelia's notes convey yet again a sense of solemn
soliloquy:

> Now and again the sun illumines mystic caves and rearing
> fortresses or shows giant cloud creatures mocking with
> lumpy paws the tiny man-made bird among them.[5]

Inadvertently, perhaps, her log for this leg of the flight
helps confirm that she was not flying her original Electra:
"Strong head winds again cut speed to an *average* [empha-
sis added] of 148 miles [per hour], which included dodging
squalls and flying low."[6] The Model 10E's normal cruising speed at optimum cruising altitude was about 140–50
miles per hour; therefore, to average 148, she would have
had to achieve a much faster speed while simultaneously
flying at low altitude and maneuvering to avoid heavy
weather. In fact, of course, the powerful Pratt & Whitney
Wasp Seniors of the Electra enabled it to fly in excess of
220 miles per hour, when necessary. Consequently, Earhart could easily attain an average speed over the ground
of 148 even while climbing, descending, and turning to
skirt the giant rain clouds.

She landed at Zandery Airfield, twenty-five miles outside Paramaribo, at 11:50 A.M. There, she would write,
"soldiers stood by to pump in gasoline from drums and to
guard the plane."[7] She and Noonan took a train over a
picturesque rail line to the Dutch colonial town. At the
Palace Hotel, where they spent the night, the navigator ran
into an old friend from his Pan American days, Carl
Doak.

June 4. A 1,628-mile flight brought them to Fortaleza,
in northeastern Brazil, where the plane's controls were

adjusted, the entire aircraft inspected, and the engine oil changed. These operations, performed gratis by Pan Am, account for an extra day spent here.

June 6. The relatively short hop of 270 miles to Parnamirio Airport at Natal, Brazil, was routine. The flyers landed at 6:55 A.M.

June 7. By dramatic contrast, the next leg was nineteen hundred miles over the Atlantic to Dakar, French Senegal, on the hump of the West African coast. The pair took off in the middle of the night from an unlighted runway. Once again, Amelia noted down a ground-speed average of about 150 miles, even though she "did not at all open up the engines."[7]

A revealing incident occurred toward the end of this long flight. Just after the plane passed over the Cape Verde Islands and neared the coast, Noonan gave Amelia a new course to Dakar that called for a southerly turn to the right at the shoreline. Amelia would hear none of it. She insisted on turning left, and so they ended up in St.-Louis, Senegal, 163 miles north of their goal.

Various accounts have suggested that weather was the cause of this diversion. Indeed, Amelia wrote in her log that many features of the coastline were partially blotted out by a thick layer of haze. But, after more than thirteen hours of flying, Amelia's fatigue was probably a factor in her misjudgment. In any event, the minor mishap illustrates her propensity to rely upon her own "hunch" instead of the more objective directions provided by Noonan over the bamboo-pole-and-clothesline communications system.

June 8. The next day, Earhart corrected her mistake by flying back along the coast to Dakar. She and Noonan decided to lay over one more day before facing the desolate, barren, and treacherous Sahel, the Central African desert south of the Sahara. (The area is probably familiar today principally as the setting for the last grueling days of the annual Paris-Dakar Rally.) It was now that the flight would leave the routes regularly used by Pan Am and other established airlines. In fact, few if any planes had ever flown over these regions of the world. The perils of a forced landing here would be as bad or worse than those of having to ditch in water.

June 9. Dangerous weather, including large areas of low atmospheric pressure with the attendant threat of tornadoes and severe sandstorms, delayed the departure from Dakar. It also convinced Earhart to change her announced destination—Niamey, in southwestern Niger—and fly instead to Gao, Mali, which was located near the northernmost extremity of the Niger River. After a flight of 1,140 miles, the Electra landed in Gao in the early afternoon.

From this point onward, Amelia Earhart begins fabricating an account that is not at all the full story. Because of numerous inconsistencies and unlikely circumstances, it is clear that the actual flight cannot be reconciled with its publicly stated aims.

Consider the following passages, which began the day before takeoff from Dakar:

Tomorrow [June 10, 1937], if all goes well, we start the long air route across Africa. Exactly what course we will fly will be determined as we progress. Extremely hot weather is creating unfavorable conditions in the interior. I am warned of tornadoes to the south and sandstorms to the north. So I must try to squeeze in between.[8]

A few paragraphs later, she claims that a last-minute decision had to be made:

I decided to shift the course slightly to the north [nearly three hundred miles], making our objective Gao on the upper reaches of the River Niger.[9]

Yet, despite this allegedly unexpected alteration in her plans, there was (as the expression goes in that part of the world) "no problem":

> . . . always we found my usual calling cards, fifty-gallon drums of gasoline, each with my name printed large upon it in white or red lettering. The exact quantity of fuel, all as arranged months before . . .[10]

She is talking about arid wastes so sparsely settled that one city in the Sahel is legendarily synonymous with the farthest end of the earth: Timbuktu. Yet precious fuel somehow swiftly appears at an airport that was not on her planned route, with her name on the barrels. Amelia claimed that Gao was provisioned because it had been selected as an alternate, but the truth is that the expedition's chart of planned landing spots and alternates (i.e., the only locations where fuel would be placed) does not include Gao.

How, then, could she know that the vagaries of weather would lead her in that direction that day, rather than to one of the planned alternate sites? To put this incident into perspective, consider that the Electra 12 was capable of carrying 1,150 gallons of fuel, or slightly more than the contents of twenty-one five-hundred-pound drums. Put another way (and quite apart from the sizable cost), this would be a shipping burden of more than 10,500 pounds. In French West African territory, the settlements were remote, the roads few and badly maintained, and camels the primary means of transporting freight. For all of these reasons, much thought had to go into where and when the voraciously thirsty Electra would appear out of the sky.

These considerations lead to another question that is central to the truth about the flight. Why did Earhart choose to direct her route across the barren, uncharted, waterless expanse of the Sahel in the first place? The announced goal of her flight was to circle the globe at the equator, but she was flying roughly thirteen to eighteen degrees north of that band. Besides, equatorial Africa was virtually festooned with towns that were well populated and English- speaking: Freetown, Port Harcourt, Stanleyville, Leopoldville, Addis Ababa, Victoria, Nairobi. Just south of the equatorial line, jungles offered a special hazard to the downed pilot, but there was no reason to fear that she would stray that far off course. Rather, the decision to fly so far north of the equator hints at a desire to avoid the prying eyes of local authorities, an intent to make reconnaissance overflights of the African desert regions, or both.

Her notes about the flight from Gao may be more revealing in this regard than she realized:

> First we followed the Niger River one hundred and seventy miles, checking over the military post at Niamey. [It is worth mentioning that this was a diversion of about 150 miles from a direct course.] Later I learned that French authorities were at the field to receive us. In retrospect I was sorry that I did not drop down to pay a call. But at the time, with weather treating us well, it seemed wise to press on.[11]

She goes on to talk about air routes through Central Africa, mentioning by the bye that both the French and the British were engaging in considerable military flying throughout the region.

> But with all that has been done, maps for the most part are far from satisfactory. This desert mid-region is a difficult country, and years of work will be required to map it well. We had the best maps available [from the U.S. military, of course], supplemented with information from pilots at each

stop. But even so, it was not easy going where we had to depend on them.[12]

For his part, Noonan would write about this route from a strictly professional point of view:

> From a navigational aspect our flights over the desert were more difficult than over water. That was because the maps of the country are very inaccurate and consequently extremely misleading. In fact, at points no dependence at all could be placed on them. Also, recognizable landmarks are few and far between, one part of the desert being as much like another as two peas in a pod. However we were lucky in always reaching our objectives. In all the distance I don't think we wandered off the course for half an hour, although there were times when I couldn't have bet a nickel on the accuracy of our assumed position.[13]

Why, then, cross Africa the hard way? Because U.S. officials knew that there would not be many more years of freedom to work on mapping the strategic regions of Central and North Africa (or, for that matter, much of the rest of the globe). In part, therefore, the sophisticated Fairchild aerial-survey cameras had been mounted in the belly of the Electra to take the photos necessary for at least cursory mapping of strategically important areas. For the kind of thorough mapping needed by military planners, it would be necessary to set up methodical, laborious, time-consuming overflights, but since Amelia's route took her nearby, why not have her veer off and take a few snapshots?

June 10. The Electra flew more than a thousand miles, passing over huge Lake Chad, the halfway point across the African continent, to land at Fort-Lamy, in Chad.

June 11. Earhart and Noonan had planned to take off at dawn to beat the Central African heat, but they were delayed by a leak in an oleo strut, a shock absorber on one of the landing gear. At about one-thirty in the afternoon, they were finally able to leave for El Fasher, French Equatorial Africa. By then, the day's accumulating heat gave them an especially rough ride, as sharp vertical shafts of superheated air rose from the arid desert floor. Significantly, they completed the seven-hundred-mile trip in slightly more three hours, a ground speed of well over two hundred miles per hour.

At El Fasher, the flyers stayed overnight with the governor of Dafur Province and his wife, whose home was a former Sultan's palace.

June 12. On the way to Massawa, Eritrea, located where the East African coast meets the Red Sea, there was an intermediate stop in Khartoum.

June 13. At Massawa, the travelers, already considerably wearied from heat, were subjected to temperatures in excess of 1 1 o degrees Fahrenheit. They spent the night in Italian-army quarters as guests of Colonel De Silvestro Luigi.

June 14. The next day, although she apparently did not know it beforehand, Amelia would set a minor new aviation record, becoming the first person to fly from the Red Sea to Karachi, in what was then still India. Early in the morning, she and Noonan lifted out over the Red Sea at its narrowest point, the entrance to Bab al-Mandab, and flew to the Arabian coast. They flew over Aden (now part of the People's Democratic Republic of Yemen), over the uninhabited expanse of the treeless, waterless, and otherwise virtually lifeless Arabian Desert, along the shoreline rather than the interior because of official restrictions, and occasionally out over portions of the Arabian Sea. They crossed the Gulf of Oman at the Tropic of Cancer and entered Asia, the fourth continent on their itinerary.

Bypassing a tentatively planned stop at Gwadar, in

southernmost Baluchistan, they pressed on to Karachi, landing at 7:00 P.M. They had covered 1,920 miles in a total flight time of thirteen hours and ten minutes. On hand to greet them was Jacques de Sibour, a Socony-Vacuum Oil Company employee who had been instrumental in setting up the logistics for the flight up to that point.

June 15. Earhart and Noonan spent the day resting from the exhausting challenges of the previous five days.

June 17. From Karachi, a truly equatorial route would have taken the flight next to Bombay, then on to Colombo, Ceylon (now Sri Lanka), which is very close to the equator, then across the Indian Ocean to Singapore, and eventually to New Guinea. All along the way, the pair could have landed in English-speaking cities.

Instead, Earhart aimed for Calcutta, taking a route over Central India, some thirteen hundred miles north of the equator. To look ahead for a moment, the route would continue to lie way off the mark, if the goal was, as stated, the world record attempt. They would be flying via Burma and Bangkok, first on a route that was extremely perilous and navigationally strange, flying over the rugged Burmese highland terrain, then down the Isthmus of Thailand.

In any event, on this day they would make Calcutta's Dum Dum Airport just after four o'clock in the afternoon, having flown 1,390 miles.

June 17. The plan was to reach Bangkok after an intermediate stop at Akyab, Burma, on the western coast of the Bay of Bengal. The day's first setback was extremely poor weather over the humid delta lands where the Ganges and Brahmaputra rivers flow into that bay. Later, after the stop at Akyab, Amelia found herself flying into a fierce monsoon. In fact, the flight had arrived in the region virtually at the height of the monsoon season. They could now expect the worst possible weather of the entire attempt. As the Electra was severely battered by the truly torrential rains, a bolt of lightning struck, disabling the radio. The pilot's description helps explain why she had to turn back to Akyab that day:

> Once in the air the elements grew progressively hostile. The wind, dead ahead, began to whip furiously. Relentless rains pelted us. The monsoon, I find, lets down more liquid per second than I thought could come out of the skies. Everything was obliterated in the deluge, so savage that it beat off patches of paint along the leading edge of my plane's wings. Only a flying submarine could have prospered. It was even wetter than in that deluge of the mid-South Atlantic.[14]

In her retreat, Amelia had to fly out over the waters of the great bay in order to avoid crashing down on the tops of the hills inland, flying so low that she was afraid she might strike the waves and be pulled under. In her notes, she leaves no doubt that she only narrowly escaped crashing.

Back in Akyab, after what Fred Norman described as "two hours and six minutes of going nowhere,"[15] she told the airport ground crew that she hoped the weather would improve by the following day. They replied that she could probably expect no change for the next three months. Recalling this incident, Amelia would write that she had missed the season of cool, dry, favorable weather "because of the Honolulu delay."[16]

This comment, of course, contradicts her public declaration earlier that the direction of this second attempt was west-to-east in order to take advantage of the season's weather. Further, the weather she now faced would include strong seasonal headwinds from the southeast—dead on her nose—for most of the rest of the planned route. Once again, conditions of the actual flight underscore the obvious: flying east to west, as on the original attempt, she would have encountered better atmospheric conditions and enjoyed a faster, safer passage along the way as well.

June 18. Despite the ground crew's warnings, they tried for Bangkok again, darting around the rain squalls of the persistent monsoon. But even Amelia's stubborn determination could not overcome the ancient, cyclical forces of nature. The weather was worse than the day before. After a tempestuous flight of only four hundred miles, they were forced to land, and remain, at Rangoon.

They amused themselves by taking an automobile trip to see the sights, accompanied by the American consul, Austin C. Brady, and a Mr. R. P. Pollard. Going down the fabled and colorful "Road to Mandalay," they were fascinated by the diversity of cultures, religions, and manners of dress, and delighted to visit the Golden Pagoda, the gold-plated domes of which had been Amelia's first glimpse of the city from the air.

June 19. Under squall-tattered skies, the flyers were able to reach Bangkok at last, make a brief fuel stop, and then fly an almost directly southerly route over the Gulf of Siam (now the Gulf of Thailand). In this region, the weather improved dramatically, and they were able to land in Singapore at 5:25 P.M. (In doing so, they won $25 from the pilot of a Dutch airliner coming out of Rangoon by beating him to the field.)

Amelia duly noted that Singapore's "magnificent new nine-million dollar airport" was "an aviation miracle of the east." But perhaps she unconsciously betrayed the undercurrents of her trip by also writing that, "from the standpoint of military strategy, Singapore is pre-eminent in the Far East . . . the cross road of trade with Europe, Africa, India, Australia, China and Japan."

She and her navigator spent the night at the home of American Consul General Monnett B. Davis and his wife.

June 21. After rising at 3:00 A.M., Earhart and Noonan left Singapore before dawn and, by flying across the Java Sea and Sumatra to Bandoeng, Dutch East Indies, left the Asian continent behind and finally returned to the equator.

June 24–27. After a three-day interlude, they headed eastward on the 24th for Surabaja, about 350 miles away, at the opposite end of the island. The next day, however, there was some undefined trouble that required them to fly back to Bandoeng for "certain further adjustments of faulty long-distance flying instruments."[17]

During this period, little was heard from Amelia and, uncharacteristically, not much more was set down in her sketchy notes. She did mention in *Last Flight* that a certain F. O. Furman, supposedly one of Lockheed's maintenance specialists, was available in Bandoeng to do an overhaul on the Electra's engines. But this is odd on several counts.

First, Amelia does not complain of engine trouble. Second, the Electra's engines, virtually brand-new and undoubtedly cared for with Earhart's well-known "kid-glove" treatment, had not yet been in service long enough for even a standard scheduled checkup, much less a major overhaul. The ordinary schedule of maintenance, which included no more than an oil change and a general inspection, was required every fifty hours of flying time. It had just taken place at Karachi. The next maintenance was scheduled for Lae.

The kind of major maintenance implied by Furman's intervention, on the order of an engine overhaul, would be necessary only in the event of major engine trouble, or after at least five hundred hours of flying time (more than twice the total projected for the entire circumnavigation). Yet the Electra's reliable Pratt & Whitney engines had run smoothly throughout the flight, so far as is known. As experts like Furman know very well, overhauling them would have been bizarre, since the chance of engine failure is much greater with newly overhauled engines than with seasoned ones. And if there *had* been an engine problem of some magnitude, it could have been handled in Singapore, at those sterling new facilities that had sent Amelia into such verbal raptures. The frontier facilities at Bandoeng, by contrast, would have been a nutty place to attempt a complicated teardown and overhaul of the Electra's radial engines.

In fact, there has never been any plausible explanation for what Furman was supposedly doing in Bandoeng. The usually informative, not to say voluble, Earhart fails us here. Engine specialist F. O. Furman, whoever he really was, probably appeared to service the Electra's secret cameras and other special equipment. Or to retrieve film. After all, as her own writing implies, Earhart had just flown over Singapore, the most famous fortress in Asia. Britain may have been a U.S. ally, but sensible nations keep tabs on their allies as well as their enemies, active or potential. Or, to take a somewhat less cynical view, perceptive American strategists may have anticipated that this part of the world was not firmly held—only five years later, in the event, Singapore was in the hands of America's adversaries, the Japanese. Quite apart from geopolitical considerations, Furman may have appeared simply to collect exposed film, check out how accurately the cameras were working, and make any necessary adjustments before the big shoot, the Japanese-held Marshall Islands.

Prudent operating procedure, in fact, would have called for a thorough inspection and testing of the espionage equipment before this critical last phase. The Electra had been tossed about by the turbulent up- and down-drafts of the Sahel and buffeted by India's torrential monsoons. It had suffered as many tough landings as smooth ones, on all manner of runway surfaces. The plane, but particularly its interior compartments, had endured the heat and billowing sand of the desert, the icy temperatures of high-altitude flight, and the drenching moisture of rain and cloud, as well as dank and drizzly salt sea air.

Aborting the Saurabaja flight for the inspection of camera equipment is much more likely than Amelia's story. In fact, the alleged difficulties with instruments and navigation aids seem to have healed themselves, for she does not explain how they were overcome.

Early charts for the flight's initially proposed itinerary suggest yet another possible explanation for Earhart's silence during this period. While she was out of touch with the world, she could easily have taken direct flights over the Marshalls by way of the Philippines. Probable as this eventuality may seem, however, it is in the realm of pure speculation.

June 27. Earhart and Noonan finally embarked from Bandoeng and reached Koepang, on the island of Timor, making the twelve-hundred-mile flight in about five hours. This route took them over the huge, gardenlike island of Java, romantic Bali, Sumbawa Island, and the Savu Sea. Since they were flying against time zones, there was not enough daylight left for them to make the long hop to Port Darwin, Australia, that day.

June 28. On a route ten to twelve degrees south of the equator, they flew the five hundred miles over the Timor Sea to Darwin, pushing strong headwinds that extended their flight time to three hours, thirty-three minutes. Conflicting accounts explain why they then stayed in Darwin for the next two days.

According to a statement issued to the press in Los Angeles, this was a bureaucratic delay because the flyers' medical clearances had not been properly issued. According to Amelia's notes, however, their required medical examinations for tropical diseases were strictly routine, if thorough, and only slightly delayed the refueling of the Electra. She does not mention any foul-up with medical clearances or, indeed, offer any other reasons why she and Noonan did not take off for two days.

The Darwin interval, however, is wholly consistent with a strange pattern that had been emerging in the progress of the flight. In the weeks prior to Bandoeng, Earhart had allowed nothing to stop or even slow her easterly progression, but, the nearer she came to the Pacific, the slower and more methodical was her advance. Delays increased and went unexplained. The flight seemed to start and stop at the whim of some unseen, inscrutable force.

June 30. After a seven-hour, forty-three-minute flight over the Arafura Sea, Earhart and Amelia landed at Lae, New Guinea. Yet again, Amelia's log shows that she was able to achieve an incredibly high average ground speed (155.5 miles per hour) against strong headwinds.[18] It can also be inferred that she was pushing the plane for speed, probably twenty to thirty miles per hour faster than on previous legs of the flight (assuming that she did indeed fly over the routes she described).

July 1. At precisely 10:00 A.M. Lae time, or 00:00 Greenwich Mean Time (GMT), the flyers began the 2,556-mile-long flight in the direction of Howland Island. This, the longest planned leg of the record flight, was by far the most hazardous.

CHAPTER EIGHT

Lost

SOS ... SOS ... SOS ... SOS ... Northwest unknown island 177 longitude ... Quite down, but
radio still working ...

   Battery very weak ... Don't know how long we
can hold out ...

   —Amelia Earhart, radio transmission, July 5, 1937

In 1937, the world was finally balanced on
the dizzying brink of cataclysmic change.
The selection of Prince Konoye as premier
of Japan virtually guaranteed a highly ag-
gressive national war policy. In response,
President Roosevelt, offering a sop to concerned isolationists in Congress and the
voters as well, signed the U.S. Neutrality
Act.

   Then occurred the "Incident at the
Marco Polo Bridge," in which Japanese soldiers fired upon the Chinese village of
Wanping. "AMERICAN SCRAP IRON PLAYS
GRIM ROLE IN FAR EASTERN WAR," roared
headlines in the U.S. The point was that
the Japanese, in violation of the Neutrality

Act, had been manufacturing armaments out of scrap metal and other commodities purchased from American suppliers. Some outraged politicians called for expansion of the act's embargo provisions, but Roosevelt was cautious. His immediate concern was the possibility that any such gesture would cause Japan to retaliate.

It was as these and related events roiled the international scene that Amelia Earhart and Fred Noonan had set off to girdle the globe.

Before dawn on the morning of July 2, the Coast Guard cutter *Itasca* lay just off Howland Island. The ship was supposed to provide radio contact as Amelia homed in toward the island, but the skipper, Commander Warner K. Thompson, was confused and exasperated. Inexplicably, the higher-ups had not explained Earhart's exact intentions, or even informed him what type of radio equipment she was using. There had been nothing like the degree of coordination and preflight briefing that would be standard for such an unproved venture.

According to one of Thompson's notations in the ship's log, radio operators were to monitor 3,105 kilocycles by day, 6,210 by night.[1] His narrative report for the period, however, indicates that he was none too sure about this, or even about the date or time of Amelia's takeoff from Lae. He had not himself been able to inform her that high-frequency radio gear was available aboard ship; consequently, all preflight planning had been made around the use of the low-frequency five-hundred-kilocycle DF. (It would turn out that Earhart had learned about the *Itasca*'s high-frequency equipment from other sources.)

At the same time, the skipper was being bombarded by conflicting information from several sources, including

George Putnam in Los Angeles, the San Francisco division of the Coast Guard, and Mrs. Ruth Hampton, assistant director of territories for the Department of the Interior. Amelia had cabled Hampton from New Guinea with details of her planned departure and the radio frequencies she intended to use.

Finally, there was Richard Blackburn Black, ostensibly aboard the *Itasca* to serve as the Earhart operation's personal representative. Publicly identified only as an employee of Interior's Division of Islands and Territories, Black had in fact been long involved in U.S. covert operations, such as the establishment of colonists and facilities on the Line Islands. He would go on to become a high-ranking officer in Naval Intelligence during the coming war and retire as an admiral.

Perhaps Thompson derived some comfort from Black's presence, but in the event the skipper could do little but simply wait, having been given a vague assignment that was definitely not "by the book."

The first message came through in the early-morning darkness. It was barely intelligible to the ship's radio operators. Only three words were understood definitively enough to be noted down in the log for 2:45 A.M.: ". . . cloudy and overcast."[2]

Because the total transmission time was very short, only a few scant seconds, a direction-finder (DF) station would not be able to take a fix. Moreover, as far as the *Itasca* was concerned, the issue was moot. According to long-classified ship's logs, the ship's DF system was inoperative. Its batteries had been allowed to "run down during the night."

A second message came exactly an hour later, at 3:45 A.M. It was more intelligible, but briskly clipped: "*Itasca* from Earhart. *Itasca* from Earhart. Overcast. Will listen on the hour and the half-hour."[3]

There followed a silence lasting two and a half hours. Meanwhile, daylight had begun to filter down through the clouds above the *Itasca*, revealing heavy swells driven by a strong easterly wind. To the northwest, in the direction of the Marshall Islands, boiled a furious squall line. This phenomenon, a narrow band of towering, active thunderstorms, is a not-too-distant cousin to the tornado. Capable of producing heavy hail and its own small tornadoes, it can be among the most violent forms of weather.

Hundreds of miles to the west, Earhart and Noonan were undoubtedly very busy during their protracted silence. By first light, they had been in the air for seventeen hours, forced to fly for the last several without being able to see the stars needed for fixing their position. Perhaps the navigator decided to wait until sunrise to calculate their location with a "sunshot."

If Noonan had wanted to take the trouble, however, he could definitely have found their relative bearing from the *Itasca*'s radio signals by using the Electra's new ADF. He could also have tried a technique called "bracketing," which involves flying perpendicular to the direction of a radio signal and noting the time taken to fly between bearings. The data can be used to calculate the distance to the signal's transmitter. In other words, Earhart and Noonan had the capability to ascertain the exact bearing and distance to a radio signal if they chose to do so.

That they did not may be indicated by the apparent scarcity and brevity of the signals Earhart sent before daylight. Perhaps they were otherwise occupied. Or perhaps they thought they might be approaching, or even flying over, forbidden territory, and did not want to give any hostile DF stations a chance to get a fix on the Electra. In fact, Earhart may have been briefed about the precise locations of Japanese DF stations. Secretly, the U.S. Navy had pinpointed them all. What Amelia's contacts did not know, however, was the actual capability of the Japanese equipment, which turned out to be far superior to any yet produced in the West.

That Earhart transmitted few messages before daylight contradicts the assumption that she became lost during the latter part of her flight from Lae. Had that been the case, she would have been compelled to try to find out her exact location by transmitting many more signals of longer duration.

Besides, one of her last messages that morning, which came at 8:44 A.M., suggests that she thought they were in the clear. She noted that they were on a "line of position" 337 degrees relative bearing northwest of Howland Island. In other words, at least at one point, they had navigated in such a way as to fly down a southeastern line toward the island. (See map, pp. 6–7.)

If Noonan had indeed waited until morning to calculate a "sunline" position, he could have located them with fair accuracy, given a sufficient and unobstructed view of the sun. The technique is essentially the same as using the position of any other star to determine location. It is also possible that they could have located themselves by spotting an identifiable island.

Either way, they were probably detected by the Japanese task force attached to the carrier *Akagi*, which was positioned off Jaluit Atoll, less than four hundred miles north of one of the known fixes of the Earhart plane. The ships were ostensibly conducting maneuvers in the area by coincidence, but it is reasonable to speculate that they had been positioned there for the express purpose of taking any action necessary to protect the nation's proprietary islands from the threat of incursion posed by the well-publicized Earhart flight. Nor is it unlikely that Earhart and Noonan would have seen the Japanese task force in the early light of dawn, or even watched the deadly flowering of anti-aircraft shells bursting in the air and the carrier-based Zeros taking off from the deck in pursuit. If so, after having flown twenty-seven thousand miles for just that purpose, they would undoubtedly have turned on the cameras.

At 6:15 A.M., Amelia reported that she was "about 200 miles out approximately" and whistled into the microphone, the universal method of giving a signal by radio so that a DF operator can get a bearing.[4]

Half an hour later, at 6:45 A.M., she sent a message that was to cause disbelief and endless debate: ". . . please take bearing on us and report in half an hour. About 100 miles out."[5]

Obviously, an airplane that actually covers a hundred miles in half an hour has a surface speed of two hundred miles per hour. It was well known that the Electra 10E, the plane Earhart started out with in Hawaii, had an optimum airspeed of only 140 miles per hour. In addition, because she was flying into a headwind, her speed over the surface would have been cut to less than that. No one knew, of course, that Earhart was actually flying an aircraft that was perfectly capable of a two-hundred-mile-per-hour speed, even with a headwind.

The apparently incredible message may have spurred the *Itasca*'s radio operators, who had been continually trying to make contact with Amelia ever since her first transmission, to try even harder. If she ever heard them, she did not respond to their questions.

The next two signals she initiated came in at the highest reading, "strength five."

At 7:42 A.M.: "We must be on you but cannot see you. Gas is running low. Have been unable to reach you by radio. Flying at 1,000 feet . . ."

At 7:46 A.M.: "We are circling but cannot see you."[6]

The reported signal strength has been the basis for further speculation. Interpreting the reading to mean that the plane's transmitter must have been very close to the ship's receiver station led to the generally accepted theory that Earhart flew to within a few miles of Howland Island that fateful morning.

Such an assumption, however, ignores a basic fact: many conditions influence the behavior of radio signals. Those broadcast in the frequency used by Earhart and the *Itasca* radiomen, for example, can travel very long distances, even under normal conditions. But radio signals will often exhibit unpredictable idiosyncrasies over the flat, reflective surface of the ocean. In certain cases, they could become "skip" waves that could be heard halfway around the world. According to many radio operators, this did in fact occur with Earhart's transmissions. Moreover, little is known, even now, about the exact specification and capabilities of the radios installed in Earhart's plane or the receivers aboard the Coast Guard ship.

For all of these reasons, no definitive conclusion about the proximity of the Electra to Howland Island can be drawn. In other words, what has been frequently presented as strong evidence—i.e., the apparent strength of the Electra's transmission signals toward the end—is actually no evidence either way.

At 8:44 A.M.: "We are in line of position 157-337 [degrees]. Will repeat this message on 6210 KC [kilocycles]. Wait. Listening on 6210. We are running north and south."[7]

This was the last time Amelia got through to the *Itasca*'s radiomen, who thought they detected anxiety in her voice. At 9:00 A.M., the point at which it was assumed her fuel supply would be exhausted, the largest sea-and-air search in history was launched. As the world knows, it did not yield a trace. What is less widely known, and may help explain the failure of the massive operation, is that the official searchers were mistaken in believing that Earhart was never heard from again after her tense 8:44 A.M. transmission.

CHAPTER NINE

SOS

She broadcast signals for four solid days.
    —Walter McMenamy, interview with author

Incredibly, the supposedly vanished Amelia Earhart continued to broadcast for days after she was downed, heard on one or more of those occasions by a relatively large number of radio operators, from the official to the unofficial, from the reliable to the wacky.

At 9:00 A.M., for example, just as the search was about to begin, Amelia was heard by a radio operator on Nauru, an island west of Howland and the Gilbert group. One phrase came through clearly on 6,210 kilocycles: "Land in sight ahead."[1]

The following day, a Pan Am radio operator on Wake Island filed an official report quoting the longest transmission yet:

SOS . . . SOS . . . SOS . . . SOS . . . Northwest unknown island 177 longitude . . . Quite down, but radio still working . . .

> Battery very weak . . . Don't know how long we can hold
> out . . . We are OK but a little wet . . . Calling [on] 3105
> kilocycles . . . Give me a long call (fade out) KHAQQ [Ame-
> lia's call letters] . . . Plane on cay northwest Howland Island
> . . . Both OK. One wing broken. Bearing 337 . . . 58 minutes
> above equator L.A.T. . . . Island 133 acres . . . Must be a new
> one.[2]

Her last remark is not so strange as it might sound:
many of the Pacific's shoals, islets, cays, and atolls were
not charted at the time. Indeed, many have not yet been
discovered and officially set down today.

According to the Pan Am operator, there was a "rip-
pling effect" in the signal, a common phenomenon when
batteries powering a radio are running low. He also heard
the sound of an engine idling in the background.[3]

The transmission lasted long enough for him to get a
DF fix showing the signal to be three to four hundred
miles northwest of Howland Island. It originated from
144 degrees true bearing from Wake, or roughly south by
southeast; the reciprocal of that, roughly north by north-
east, was very close to the 337 degrees from Howland
reported by Amelia as her position.

Still other pleas for help were heard off and on for several days. As Walter McMenamy recalled, "Amelia
broadcast a series of dashes—a prearranged signal to indicate that she was down on land—as well as a voice message
that she was down approximately 281 miles northwest of
Howland. She broadcast signals for four solid days."[4]

His recollection seems confirmed by a dispatch in the
July 6 edition of the *New York Times*:

> The fliers were told to send a series of two long dashes if they
> were on the water, and a series of three long dashes if they
> were on land. Paul Mantz, technical adviser to Miss Earhart

when she was making her globe-circling flight plans, said three long dashes, as requested by the Pan American station in Honolulu, had been heard by him in Los Angeles.

Radio operators in Honolulu and elsewhere also reported hearing the series of three dashes.

Why, then, did no one go out there and find her?

Someone did.

But Commander Thompson of the *Itasca* did not find the downed Electra, for he was not blessed with our recently sharpened hindsight. Nor, since the Coast Guard was a civilian auxiliary, not part of the U.S. Navy, would he have been privy to Naval Intelligence information. Finally, he was probably not within the select circle of those who had been informed about the true nature of this leg of the Earhart flight. It appears that he was not even certain she would be approaching Howland from the northwest.

If he or his crew learned about any of Amelia's transmissions subsequent to the 8:44 A.M. signal logged by his radio operators, he never revealed it. For one thing, he and other participants in the air-and-sea search kept their radios busy staying in touch with each other and coordinating their efforts. For another, the official reaction to reports of transmissions heard after July 2 was to try to undermine their credibility. Little information gleaned from them seems to have been passed along to the searchers. Not until half a century later would all of the reported messages be brought together and the authentic ones sorted out from among those that were honest mistakes or outright hoaxes.

Yet Commander Thompson did make some shrewd guesses based upon the little he knew for certain. For example, he reasoned that the "position" Amelia mentioned in her 8:44 A.M. transmission was Howland Island and "157-337" meant a true bearing of 157 degrees from her plane to the island, or 337 degrees (the opposite of 157 degrees) from the island to her.[5] In other words, the phrase "We are in line of position 157-337" indicated that, just as the *Itasca* lost contact, and minutes before the Electra was due to run out of fuel, she was somewhere north-northwest of Howland. To interpret the numbers in reverse would have placed her south-southeast of the island, but the skipper rejected that possibility, which would have put her thirty miles away, near Baker Island, which she could have recognized from the air, or possibly Winslow Reef, visible to the east of Howland. Besides, he believed that the strength of her signal showed that she was closer than either of those two spots. Therefore, Thompson decided to head north, skirting the heavy squall line; he deduced that Earhart had been on the other side of it at one point.

By July 3, a huge task force was coming from Hawaii and the U.S. mainland to join in the search. It included the aircraft carrier USS *Lexington*, which carried ninety-eight planes ready to comb the Pacific (almost twice the number given in the press at the time). The same day, the involvement and concern of the president were reported in the *New York Times*:

HYDE PARK, NY—President Roosevelt kept in close touch with the Navy Department today, seeking information on the fate of Amelia Earhart. White House officials said he talked with the Naval Operations Office many times by telephone.

Joining immediately with the *Lex* were the destroyers *Drayton*, *Lamson*, and *Cushing*, the fuel tanker *Ramapo*, and the minesweeper *Swan*. The battleship *Colorado* caught up with the group soon afterward. By the way, in rushing to the search area, the *Lexington* reportedly reached an incredible, record-breaking speed of thirty-three knots. The previous record had been held by the French liner *Normandie*, which had only briefly attained a top speed of thirty-two knots before her skipper cautiously eased off the turbines. The second-place *Queen Mary* had averaged 30.63 knots on her best crossing.

More astonishing than this feat of speed, however, was the initial deployment of the task force, which went straight to Canton Island, in the Phoenix group, some four hundred miles southwest of Howland Island. The *Itasca* was already searching the area two hundred miles north of Howland, accompanied now by HMS *Moorsby*, a British freighter. But, inexplicably, the main task force proceeded with a search of the islands and waters of the Phoenix archipelago, launching planes from the *Lex* and landing shore parties, before finally giving up and joining the search around Howland.

Or perhaps this behavior was not so inexplicable, after all. If Amelia's 8:44 A.M. message had been interpreted exactly opposite to Commander Thompson's reading, her position would indeed have been more or less in the direction of some of the islands in the Phoenix group. Much more likely, however, is that the deployment shows that certain navy officials knew that Amelia had planned to land at Canton or a neighboring airfield all along. Her publicly announced plan to land on Howland, in that case, had been nothing but an excuse for the U.S. to build an airfield there.

At the very least, the inner circle knew from Naval Intelligence that the Electra carried a fourteen-hundred-mile fuel reserve. Contrary to what Thompson believed, it could stay aloft for several hours past 9:00 A.M. Of course, the Coast Guard skipper could have been misled; cer-

tainly reports issuing from the Earhart operations in Los
Angeles purposely gave the public the false impression
that Amelia would have run out of fuel at that hour. If the
leaders of the search task force knew otherwise, they
would logically surmise that she could have overshot the
Howland area by several hundred miles.

Meanwhile, the U.S. and British ships were joined in
their task by a third force, as Japanese ships steamed into
the area where Amelia had last been heard by the *Itasca*.
Based upon intercepts of Japanese radio broadcasts and
other sources, Pan Am was able to report to U.S. Naval
Intelligence that both the survey ship *Koshu* and the seaplane tender *Kamoi* were operating some four to six hundred miles northwest of Howland, or roughly in the area
between Tarawa in the Gilbert Islands and Mili Atoll in
the Marshalls.[6] U.S. Navy documents affirm that the Japanese Navy Ministry sent orders to its 12th Squadron,
which operated throughout the Marshall Islands, to send
the *Kamoi* with its large seaplanes to search for Earhart's
aircraft.[7] As (Japanese) luck would have it, the vessel,
under the command of Captain Kanade Kosaka, was con-
veniently located at the time just south of Jaluit, near the
southeastern tip of the Marshalls. Similarly, the *Koshu*,
commanded by Captain Kanjiro Takagi, happened to be
positioned in the southeastern Marshalls, just northwest
of Howland, and was ordered to search that area.[8]

Even more significant, three unnamed destroyers at Jaluit formed a screen for a heavy Japanese aircraft carrier.
The presence of the formidable *Akagi* prevented U.S. officials from thinking, as it were, about taking their own
search operations into the Marshalls, even though the
southeastern boundary of the chain was a mere 250 miles
northwest of Howland and they desperately wanted to get
a glimpse of the alleged Japanese military buildup for
themselves. Despite the certainty of rejection, however, a

formal request for permission to enter the area was swiftly sent through diplomatic channels, effectively delaying a search in the most likely areas.⁹ Just as swiftly, the Japanese specifically and firmly denied entry, but said that they would themselves search their own islands. This set of circumstances was probably the single most important factor leading to the disappearance of Earhart and Noonan.

Unable to search near the Marshalls, the U.S. Navy task force did widen their efforts immediately to the south to include Britain's Gilbert Islands. It was known that Amelia had flown directly over two islands in the group, Nauru and Tarawa. In fact, she had reported sighting the Nauru light, which is located well north of a direct-line course from Lae to Howland. It was at Tarawa that the *Itasca* finally gave up the search and got permission to return to Pearl Harbor.

Largely unnoticed amid the welter of other major headlines on page 2 of the July 6 edition of the *New York Times* was a tiny box item:

DIRECTION FINDER IS USED TO PLACE EARHART PLANE

WASHINGTON, July 5—A message [from the *Itasca*] to Coast Guard Headquarters today said that the interception of "ragged" radio signals "indicate possibility Earhart plane still afloat 281 miles north of Howland Island."

The message said that bearings taken with a Coast Guard radio direction finder on Howland confirmed the approximate position of the Earhart plane indicated by the garbled radio signals, which were received earlier by the naval station at Honolulu.

The *Itasca* also reported the Howland Island station heard a radio signal with the call letters of the plane.[10]

The *Itasca* off Howland Island, Pan American Airways on Wake Island, the U.S. Navy in Honolulu, the Coast Guard Station at San Francisco, Walter McMenamy, Karl Pierson, Guy Dennis, Paul Mantz, George Palmer Putnam in Los Angeles—all heard the messages sent by Earhart and Noonan reporting that they were down on land "approximately 281 miles northwest" of Howland.

The only ships in that area were Japanese.

The official U.S. search was eventually called off as futile. As indeed it was, since the Electra had been forced down far from the area encompassed by the search.

How do we know?

From the time on July 5, 1937, when the *Itasca* disclosed that its radiomen had received and calculated the location of the Earhart radio signals northwest of Howland, to the time fifty years later when all of the reports of radio signals and position fixes were analyzed and correlated by this investigation, much new, definitive information has come to light. We know that Amelia Earhart's Electra was capable of greater speeds and longer range than was known at the time. We know these factors contributed to erroneous assumptions on the part of search coordinators and later investigators. We know that Amelia could have flown back northwest on her stated course of 337 degrees for several hours, if necessary, to return to where she and Noonan had last sighted land. We know that U.S. forces engaged in the search could not and did not search the area beyond two hundred miles northwest of Howland Island; and, finally, we know that the Japanese *were* there in considerable force, waiting, listening, monitoring the radio transmissions and the progress of the flight. It is no exaggeration to say that Amelia flew into the midst of a major Japanese naval exercise then under way in the southeastern Marshalls, made up of at least three destroyers, one battleship, one seaplane tender, and the supercarrier *Akagi*.

Now that we know these facts, fifty years after the event, it seems conceivable that Earhart and Noonan might have flown to within two hundred miles of How-land, then backtracked on the 157-337 sunline course when they did not immediately see the tiny island. At that point, their fuel would be low, though, if not critically so. It is equally conceivable that they never got closer than two to three hundred miles.

Faced with fuel exhaustion or the continued obscuring of the surface by bad weather, no experienced oceanic flyer would have wasted another drop of precious fuel in looking for the missed landfall. Certainly Earhart and Noonan, the most experienced of all, would have fol-lowed logical, standard practice and turned instantly toward an alternate landfall. If there was enough fuel remaining, they would have returned to one they had al-ready located. It can safely be assumed, for example, that they had just flown over other islands at this point, includ-ing the Marshalls. Their only rational option was to fly back toward this chain.

Here appears a curious fact that historians have missed over the decades because of a lack of familiarity with avia-tion practice: despite the long odds of finding a landfall as small as Howland Island, no alternate plan was ever pub-licly announced or even discussed. The subject is glaringly omitted from the writings collected for Amelia's book *Last Flight*, even though this is one of the fundamentals of flight planning. Every pilot selects an alternate destination before taking off; the longer the flight, the greater the num-ber of alternate plans made. It would not be unprece-dented for the Howland Island area to be obscured by fogs or clouds. Or for one of the Electra's engines to fail, or for a fuel tank to spring a leak, or for a radio to fail. Scores of possible eventualities might make them unable to find the island, as they well knew. What then? Evidently, Earhart's alternative plan was kept secret, or, as has been suggested earlier, she never intended to land at Howland as "plan A" in the first place.

Whatever her exact location early that morning, she had been tagged as an intruder and stirred up a hornet's nest. Long before daylight, when she passed over the forbidden Marshalls, fighter pilots on the *Akagi* were ordered out to search for a twin-engine American plane. As one of them would state decades later, they were not told that the pilot was a world-famous aviatrix, only that a foreigner had violated imperial-Japanese airspace and was to be forced down one way or another.[5]

When the Electra turned back toward the islands, the search was in full cry. Pilots who spotted the distinctive twin-tailed, twin-engined bright-silver monoplane instantly recognized their quarry.

The pilot who actually forced down Amelia Earhart made one warning fly-by, but the intruder plane failed to respond. On the next pass, he fired his guns. He would report that he could not be sure whether or not he made a hit, but the plane swerved downward and landed on a cay or sandspit near a larger island or atoll.

The Japanese were not under pressure to move swiftly to pick up the intruders. They knew where they were and could fix the position precisely as Amelia continued to broadcast for help. No one else was about to enter the area unannounced, and the American search party had been warned to stay away. The Japanese ships could take a while to reach the tiny island, which was probably uncharted, or, as Amelia described it in one of her transmissions, "a new one." Even if the island was on the charts, other potential rescuers might not have been helped all that much, whether they thought it a likely spot or not. Howland Island, for instance, was then shown to be more than five miles from the position later set down in U.S. Navy hydrographic surveys.*

The big problem for anyone trying to beat the Japanese to the spot, however, would be the sheer immensity of the ocean, as is shown clearly by an incident during the U.S. task-force search. Officials decided that Winslow Reef, a few miles east of Howland, and a particular sandbar charted near the reef, were likely possibilities as Amelia's forced landing place. But the aircraft sent searching from the USS *Lexington* never found either of these known, charted landmasses.

In any event, the Japanese had the field to themselves and found Earhart and Noonan on July 5, the day of her last known radio transmission. Radio reports of the capture were intercepted by operators in Hawaii and on the U.S. mainland, including Walter McMenamy. Soon afterward, according to the evidence, President Roosevelt, Eugene Vidal, and Henry Morgenthau, Jr., learned what had happened.

"He must be at least an admiral," Amelia exclaimed in her final message that day.[6] According to McMenamy, she was describing a Japanese shore patrol that was nearing the crashed Electra just before her radio fell silent at last. (Later, it would seem clear that the patrol had been sent from the seaplane tender *Kamoi*.)

---

*Like much of the rest of the Pacific, the area has not been completely charted to this day. Quite possibly, I discovered the island of Earhart's misadventure in 1982, aided by the space-age technology of a Landsat III aerial-reconnaisance satellite photograph and the bemused good nature of the pilot of a Boeing 727 jet.

Long before July 18, when the ship sent to protect Earhart, the *Itasca*, steamed back toward Pearl Harbor, she and Noonan were prisoners and well on their way, albeit via a circuitous route, to the headquarters of the Japanese Pacific Central Command on Saipan.

CHAPTER TEN

Found

And there was a female with him wearing trousers like a man, and a shirt with a scarf. She was about five feet eight inches tall.

—Bilimon Amaron, interview with author

Bilimon Amaron is now a merchant on Majuro, an island in the Marshalls not far from Jaluit Atoll. In July 1937, however, he was a health aide to a Japanese physician on Jaluit Island and was summoned to the *Kamoi* to treat a man and a woman who had been picked up on a reef near Mili Atoll.

> Sometime during the summer of 1937, we were called out to one of the Japanese military-cargo ships. I was then working as a health aide to the Japanese civilian doctor at the military hospital on Jaluit Atoll. Our director of health services was a Japanese military man. We went together to this ship and we saw a white man. He was wounded, right in front of his head and also his leg. And there was a female with him wearing trousers

like a man, and a shirt with a scarf. She was about five feet eight inches tall. The crew of the ship said they picked them up between the Gilbert Islands and Mili Island, on a small atoll. We treated the man—I personally did. The wound on the front side of the head was not very serious, but the wound around the knee was kind of a four-inch cut, inflamed, slightly bleeding; it was infected and had been open for quite a long time. I could not stitch it but used Paraply on the knee. The head wound required only a bandage. The Japanese on board told me that they had run out of fuel and came down near Mili; the man hurt himself when the plane landed.[1]

Describing the incident during an interview in June 1984, Bilimon Amaron recalled that the Japanese navy had been taking an exercise in the area at the time of the crash. The crewmen of the cargo ship were military, not civilian, he remembered, and there were guards aboard as well. The wounded man and the woman were not being treated as spies, however.

In fact, Amaron found nothing memorable about the event except the race of the marooned pair. He saw no other Caucasians in the Marshalls during those years. At the time, he had never heard of Amelia Earhart. Only much later did he recognize her and Noonan from photographs and realize what he had actually seen that day.

[I] observed Earhart sitting on a deck chair. She seemed well, smiled a few times, made no demands on anyone, and did not seem to be afraid or alarmed about her present situation. It was the Japanese crew which appeared to be more excited about the fact that a woman pilot was flying the plane.

The crew further mentioned that the flyers were returning home from Howland Island. Unable to find it in bad weather, on their way back to the Gilberts they got lost in heavy weather.[2]

According to Amaron, the pair did not leave the ship during the twenty-four hours it was docked at Jaluit. Then the *Kamoi* left for Kwajalein and, according to rumors he heard later, the pair were flown to Saipan because they were spies. He heard nothing more about their fate.

But two brothers working for the Japanese on the docks at Taroa, in the northern part of Maloelap Atoll, happened to learn more of the story.

According to John and Dwight Heine, the *Kamoi* stopped at Taroa, the easternmost and most thoroughly equipped of all Japanese marine-aviation facilities at the time, after leaving Jaluit. In an interview in May 1982, on Majuro, where the brothers live now, they recalled that they helped unload an airplane missing one wing onto the long dock at Taroa while its Caucasian flyers, a woman and a man, stayed aboard ship.[3]

John Heine, an attorney who served as a diplomat during the early days of Marshallese independence in the 1960s, also remembered what happened afterward:

> The twin-engined plane was taken off the wharf and rolled to where the airplane hangars and shops were. Much later, when the Americans started bombing, the island's commander, Admiral Tomada, had this airplane moved farther toward the interior of the island and placed in the underground hangar built for the admiral's airplane.[4]

The admiral, not a pilot, had added a second seat to a Zero fighter, his sole means of transportation to and from the island. Sometime in 1943–44, when the U.S. Army Air Corps began bombing Taroa, Tomada ordered his aircraft placed beneath a concrete revetment in his especially secure underground-storage place. The fuselage of the Electra, with the remaining wing removed, was also trundled down inside for safekeeping.

Before that, however, the U.S. Navy, in the normal course of bombing operations in the sweep toward Japan, had taken aerial photographs of the island. Of course, analysts were looking for operational fighters, bombers, torpedo planes—the weapons that the Japanese could still employ against the advancing Allied forces. Only someone specifically looking for Earhart's unique aircraft would have recognized it.[5]

Eventually, Taroa was neutralized by bombardment and bypassed by the Allies on their way to Tokyo. The island was never occupied by U.S. troops, and there is little indication that any outsiders have been there since the last Japanese went home after their nation surrendered. The ultimate fate of the Electra fuselage hidden there with such care is still unknown.

For one thing, the tiny island is treacherous to explore, despite its outward tranquillity. A number of the native inhabitants have been killed as they have stumbled upon unexploded bombs and other ammunition left from the war. Protected by the dangerous explosives, as well as by the isolation and unchanging weather, many of the above-ground buildings remain virtually as they were in 1945. It is safe to assume that the underground facilities are equally unchanged. Sitting in one of them, in all probability, right alongside Admiral Tomada's unusual two-seater Zero, is the fuselage of a Lockheed Electra, perhaps still containing the sixty-five hundred first-day-of-issue philatelic covers, now with an estimated value of over $25 million.

Saipan, one of the Mariana Islands, lies 2,660 statute miles north of Howland, 1,520 miles directly north of Lae. It has been a focal point in the mystery of Amelia Earhart.

The island was the headquarters of Nanyo Kohatsu Kaisha (the South Seas Development Corporation), the civilian organization that had aroused Allied suspicion that it was a cover for Japan's military construction throughout the Mandates. Indeed, it was. On Saipan, its holdings included a territorial military post and, in the town of Garapan, a military prison. During the war, the island would become headquarters for Japanese military operations in the Marianas.

In 1960, U.S. Air Force Major Joe Gervais and Captain Robert Dinger, who had heard rumors circulating through U.S. military channels that the Japanese had brought Earhart and Noonan to Saipan, conducted scores of interviews on the island.[6] Not long afterward, Fred Goerner, a reporter for CBS radio based in San Francisco, also conducted extensive interviews.[7]

The results of the two investigations were identical:

Over a hundred of the Chamorro natives who lived there in 1937 stated that they had seen two Americans matching the descriptions of Earhart and Noonan on the island during July and August of that year. Most were told by their Japanese captors, or heard through the tropical grapevine, that these two white persons had been caught spying. The shared assumption was that the accused spies had been executed or died on Saipan.

One of Major Gervais's interviewees was Thomas Blas, a Saipan police officer in 1960–62.[8] He reluctantly admitted that he had not only seen the Americans but also had in his possession four photographs from the period, including shots of the woman flyer. (Like many Saipanese, he referred to her casually as "Tokyo Rosa.") Blas told his story in the presence of a highly respected Guamanian police chief, José Quintinella, and his deputy, Lieutenant Eddie Camacho. Significantly, he said that he had once seen Earhart riding in a Japanese military-staff automobile with Admiral Miamoto, island governor of Saipan, in

September, but did not take a photograph of that encounter.

He was wary, and with good reason. Blas recalled that he had been working at a construction site near Tanapag Harbor and Aslito Airfield in 1937 and was made well aware then how dangerous it would be to talk to anyone about the mysterious strangers. Even years later, he remained nervous about the subject, evidently uncertain just what foreign element Major Gervais might represent. Besides, the island's long history of submission to foreign occupiers has created a well-conditioned fear about saying the wrong thing. The especially harsh, authoritarian labor state instituted by the Japanese left deep scars throughout the islands.

At first, therefore, Blas would not let Gervais look at his photographs. Finally, he hesitantly agreed to let the American see two of the four pictures. These did not show Earhart but Japanese officers who, according to Blas, were involved in bringing the alleged spies to Saipan. The policeman claimed that his other two photos showed Amelia in captivity at Garapan, but he refused to produce them. Not anticipating much success, the major left his U.S. address with Blas, just in case he ever changed his mind.[9]

Years passed.

On January 15, 1980, Gervais received a blue official business envelope of the U.S. Trust Territories of the Pacific, Mariana Islands, postmarked Saipan on January 8. There was no letter or written explanation inside, only an aged photograph (see illus. 10), cracked at one corner and yellowing around the edges. It was a shocking picture of Amelia Earhart in ravaged condition; her hands appeared to be bound in back.[10]

This was the photograph Thomas Blas had been afraid to give up two decades before, fearing reprisal. It is tangible, graphic evidence that Earhart survived beyond July 2, 1937.

But it was not the only photograph or document that offered such proof when the Americans occupied Saipan in 1944. According to the September 10 issue of *American Weekly* that year, soldiers found a pouch containing photos of Amelia.

A similar report appeared decades later in the September 1987 issue of the *Sixth Marine Division News*, based upon the recollections of Robert E. Wallack, who now lives in Woodbridge, Connecticut. Wallack was a machine gunner assigned to "D" Company, 29th Marines, when they came ashore at the village of Charon Kanoa. Somewhere near Garapan, the invaders entered a Japanese building that had been bombed. Beneath a pile of rubble, Wallack discovered a locked safe. A demolition expert applied gel explosive and blew it open. Inside was a startling cache of documents, as Wallack would recall:

> After the smoke cleared, I grabbed a brown leather attaché case with a large handle and a flip lock. The contents were official-looking papers all concerning Amelia Earhart: maps, permits and reports apparently pertaining to her around the world flight. I wanted to retain this as a souvenir, but my Marine buddies insisted that it may be important and should be turned in. I went down to the beach where I encountered a naval officer and told of my discovery. He gave me a receipt for the material, and said that it would be returned to me if it were not important. I have never seen the material since.

There are other indications that the U.S. government knew that the Japanese had captured Earhart and Noonan. Richard Blackburn Black, whom we last met on the *Itasca*, states categorically that this was known and passed through military channels. Secretary of the Treasury

Henry Morgenthau, Jr., whose department oversaw the Coast Guard, received a full report on what had happened to the pair, shortly after they supposedly disappeared.[11]

Mrs. Katherine Smith, then married to Eugene Vidal, has confirmed that her husband and others in FDR's inner circle also knew:

> Gene knew the whole thing and he told me about it. About Noonan being drunk, and the project [sic] they were doing and their capture by the Japanese. The administration knew about it.[12]

So far as is known, however, White House officials reacted to their knowledge in only one way: they suppressed the information. As should be clear from what has gone before, there was little they could do. The outbreak of war, of course, brought even greater limitations on possible action to find out more about Earhart and Noonan, or to wangle their release. Indeed, many American VIP prisoners were held by the Japanese until the end of the war, including Major General Jonathan M. Wainwright and Colonel Greg "Pappy" Boynton.

Where were Earhart and Noonan during this period? After Saipan, the trail grows cold until late in the war. At that point, developments suggest, there may have been good reason for Blas and other natives of Saipan to refer to her as "Tokyo Rosa."

7. This photograph of the Lockheed Electra, taken at March Army Air Base in southern California, is significant because it shows the aircraft under military guard, and being serviced with fuel, which contradicts U.S. government claims that Amelia Earhart's world flight was "strictly a civilian affair." *Military Branch, National Archives, Washington, D.C.*

8. A photograph, discovered at Hickham Field, Hawaii, many years after her disappearance, appears to show Amelia Earhart being sworn in to the U.S. Army Air Forces by an unknown officer as other officers look on. The officer standing behind Amelia at far left is Major General Oscar Westover, who in 1937 was the commanding officer of the USAAF. *U.S. Army*

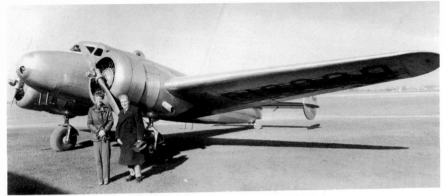

9. Amelia in front of Lockheed Electra with presidential adviser Bernard Baruch. According to Earhart aide Margo de Carrie, Baruch was in California for the purpose of persuading Amelia to cooperate with the president's plans for Pacific reconnaissance. *National Archives, Washington, D.C.*

10. A Saipanese native claims he took this photograph on Saipan in September 1937, four months after Earhart's disappearance. The man, who was still living on Saipan as late as the early 1980s, declined to relinquish the photograph to investigator Major Joseph Gervais (USAF ret.) during an interview on Saipan in the 1970s, fearing official reprisal, but later mailed the photograph to Gervais in an envelope bearing a Saipan postmark. *Courtesy Joe Gervais*

11. Marshallese natives told of Earhart and Noonan, with their Lockheed Electra aircraft, being taken aboard the Japanese seaplane tender *Kamoi*. The Heine brothers, John and Dwight, told investigators that they helped unload the Electra, missing the wing that Amelia's radio transmissions indicated was "broken," at the island of Taroa where the Japanese had secretly constructed an illegal air base. This USAAF reconnaissance photograph, taken during the bombing of the island in 1944, shows the distinctive twin-tailed monoplane, with one wing missing, sitting on a concrete revetment. The Japanese built no twin-tailed monoplanes, either before or during World War II. Taroa Island was never occupied by U.S. forces. *Military Branch, National Archives, Washington, D.C.*

Mr. Morgenthau says that he can't give
out any more information than was given
to the papers at the time of the search
of Amelia Earhart

It seems they have confidential information which would completely ruin the
reputation of Amelia and which he will
tell you personally some time when you
wish to hear it.

He suggests writing this man and telling
him that the President is satisfied
from his information, and you are too,
that everything possible was done.

-16-

H.M.Jr: And I'm not going to keep quiet.

(On White House phone) Oh, hello. - Oh, thanks.
Hello, Tommy (Malvina Scheider). How are you?
This letter that Mrs. Roosevelt wrote me about
trying to get the report on Amelia Earhart. Now,
I've been given a verbal report. If we're going to
release this, it's just going to smear the whole
reputation of Amelia Earhart, and my ..... -
Yes, but I mean if we give it to this one man we've
got to make it public; we can't let one man see it.
And if we ever release the report of the Itasca
on Amelia Earhart, any reputation she's got is gone,
because - and I'd like to - I'd really like to
return this to you.

(Continuing) Now, I know what Navy did, I know what
the Itasca did, and I know how Amelia Earhart
absolutely disregarded all orders, and if we ever
release this thing, goodbye Amelia Earhart's
reputation. Now, really - because if we give the
access to one, we have to give it to all. And my
advice is that - and if the President ever heard
that somebody questioned that the Navy hadn't made
the proper search, after what those boys went
through - I think they searched, as I remember it,
50,000 square miles, and every one of those planes
was out, and the boys just burnt themselves out
physically and every other way searching for her.
And if - I mean I think he'd get terribly angry if
somebody - because they just went the limit, and so
did the Coast Guard. And we have the report of all
those wireless messages and everything else, what
that woman - happened to her the last few minutes.
I hope I've just got to never make it public, I mean.
- O.K. - Well, still if she wants it, I'll tell
her - I mean what happened. It isn't a very nice
story. - Well, yes. There isn't anything additional to something like that. You think up a good
one. - Thank you. (Conversation ends)

(To Chauncey) Just send it back.

Chauncey: Sure.

H.M.Jr: I mean we tried - people want us to search again

12. This telephone transcript is excerpted from the Henry Morgenthau, Jr., diaries kept at the FDR Presidential Library at Hyde Park. The accompanying note was written by Malvina Scheider, secretary to Eleanor Roosevelt, to Mrs. Roosevelt, indicating Morgenthau's refusal to furnish a report of what actually happened to Amelia Earhart and Fred Noonan. *Franklin D. Roosevelt Library, Hyde Park, N.Y.*

those islands, after what we have gone through. You (Gibbons) know the story, don't you?

Gibbons: We have evidence that the thing is all over, sure. Terrible. It would be awful to make it public.

H.M.Jr: Well, the only thing that out of this - I want you (Lonigan) to check up with Social Security. Archie, give this (photostat of WPA figures) to her and let her check, and Ed, you check the legislation, will you please?

Foley: Yes. Here's an unsigned memorandum.

H.M.Jr: Excuse me?

Foley: There is what Dan said about the law.

H.M.Jr: And you two can be excused, please - Miss Lonigan and Mr. Foley.

Lonigan: Mr. Secretary, there is one factor you might wish. Yesterday Mr. Gill called it to you - the average weekly payment for direct relief was $21 a week, and I checked on what F.E.R.A. was paying in 1935, and they had full control of general relief and they paid $7.12 a week. That's the discrepancy.

H.M.Jr: Is that a family or person?

Lonigan: Everything is the family.

Haas: That's a United States average.

Lonigan: No, I think it's the city of Cleveland.

H.M.Jr: Well, it's four and a half now.

Lonigan: They mean the maximum you'd need for full programs.

H.M.Jr: I know. I mean - well, as I recall, it was around $28 a month.

Lonigan: A dollar a day.

H.M.Jr: Those figures are all drilled in my brain. I never forget them. I don't know what his object was.

(Lonigan and Foley leave)

THE WHITE HOUSE
WASHINGTON

*July 26
file*

7/20/37

MEMORANDUM FOR   THE PRESIDENT

Gene Vidal has been in very close touch
with the Earhart story, talking several times
a day to her husband, Mr. Putnam. #

He has some very interesting sidelights
and some speculations, which are probably true,
as to what actually happened. You might find
it interesting to spend 15 minutes with him.

*P.P.F.
960*

M. H. M.

*Mac
I would like to
see him for 5 or
10 minutes*

*will be back
July 26*

13. Presidential aide Marvin H. MacIntyre's memo, with the president's handwritten response, indicates that there was interest at the highest level in the fate of the downed flyers, two days after the search was called off. Three days later, on July 23, 1937, the subject again arose in a Cabinet meeting when Secretary Daniel Roper read a plaintive telegram from George Palmer Putnam, requesting the navy to search in the Maloelap Atoll area, and to ask the British and the Japanese to assist. A transcript of the Cabinet meeting states: "It was decided to ask our own and their officers to keep a lookout, but that we could not intensively search the area mentioned since we did not have the ships there." *Franklin D. Roosevelt Library, Hyde Park, N.Y.*

DEPARTMENT OF COMMERCE
BUREAU OF AIR COMMERCE

Commerce No. NR-16020
Serial No. 1055
Date 5-19-37
Approved—Disapproved—Reinspect.
_____ Inspector.

AIRCRAFT INSPECTION REPORT

Owner _____ AMELIA EARHART.

Address _____ 50 W. 45th St. New York, N.Y.

Original license—Renewal—Export—Alteration (submit drawings)—Special. After accident of _____ (Date)
(Circle which)

Manufacturer Lockheed Aircraft Corp. _____ Model 10E Spec. Specification No. 590

Open Cabin—Amphibian—Landplane—Seaplane—Flying boat—Biplane—Monoplane—Autogiro—Glider.
(Circle which)

ENGINES

MANUFACTURER	LOCATION	MODEL	SPEC. NO.	SERIAL NO.	H.P.
Pratt & Whitney	L.H.	S3H1	143	6150	550
" "	R.H.	"	"	6149	550

PROPELLER					HUB—SPEC. NO. 257		BLADES—SPEC. No 301	

MANUFACTURER	LOCATION	MATERIAL	Model	Serial No.	Model	Serial No.
Hamilton Standard	L.H. (Con. Spd)	Metal	12D-40	26534	6095A-6	66570-71
" "	R.H. " "	"	"	26533	"	65672-73

Number of fuel tanks 12 — 2 @ 81, 2 @ 16, 2 @ 102, in wing stubs. Total 1151 gal.
Location and capacity of each — 2 @ 118, 3 @ 149, 1 @ 70 in fuselage. Total oil capacity 80 in 4 tanks

Passenger seats actually provided 0 Crew 4 Are dual controls installed? Yes Removable? No

Weight empty as equipped—Actual—Computed _____ pounds. Gross weight _____ pounds.
(Circle which)

Maximum payload _____ pounds with fuel of _____ gallons.

Maximum pay load _____ pounds with full fuel tanks of _____ gallons.

Cargo space—Location and capacity of each none

Are compartments placarded for loads as shown? _____

Restrictions Restricted to long distant flights. Only bona fide members of the crew
to be carried.

ALL EQUIPMENT AND WEIGHTS thereof included in empty weight MUST BE SHOWN.

Engine ring cowl _____ lb.	Flares and holders _____ lb.	Fire extinguisher _____ lb.
Starter (type?) _____ lb.	Location _____	Heater _____ lb.
Generator _____ lb.	Radio _____ lb.	Toilet equipment _____ lb.
Wheel streamlines _____ lb.	Location _____	_____ lb.
Battery _____ lb.	Radio bonding _____ lb.	_____ lb.
Location _____	Radio shielding _____ lb.	_____ lb.
Landing lights _____ lb.	Water container _____ lb.	_____ lb.

If inspection after accident, underscore classification which applies:
1. Major repair (see Aero. Bulletin 7-H—Current Issue). Attach Form 466.
2. Minor repair (see Aero. Bulletin 7-H—Current Issue).

IMPORTANT.—All questions must be fully answered. O. K. or check marks will not be accepted. Disapprovals must show
specific defects

11—11592   20 [OVER]

a

THIS LICENSE MUST BE PROMINENTLY DISPLAYED IN THE AIRCRAFT

C   UNITED STATES OF AMERICA
DEPARTMENT OF COMMERCE
BUREAU OF AIR COMMERCE

THIS AIRCRAFT MAY BE FLOWN ONLY BY
U. S. LICENSED PILOTS

RESTRICTED Aircraft License No. NR16020   Serial No. 1055

Passengers NONE   Engine 2 WASP S3H1'S 550 HP

Model LOCKHEED ELECTRA 10-E 2 PCLM   A. T. C. — —

Weight empty as equipped — — lbs. Gross weight (Not to be exceeded) 10500 lbs.

Maximum pay load is — — lbs. with fuel of — — gals.

Maximum pay load is — — lbs. with full fuel tanks 1151 gals.

Cargo space: Location and capacity — — RESTRICTED FOR SCIENTIFIC RESEARCH AND SPECIAL FLIGHTS NO PERSONS MAY BE CARRIED EXCEPT BONA-FIDE MEMBERS OF THE CREW
THIS CERTIFIES, that the aircraft described above is a civil aircraft of the United States of America and is licensed for a period of twelve months, unless the Secretary of Commerce otherwise directs. It is licensed and registered as follows:

AMELIA EARHART 50 WEST 45TH STREET
NEW YORK NEW YORK

Unless sooner suspended or revoked, this license expires AUGUST 15 1937

Assistant Director of Air Commerce

Any alteration of this license is punishable by fine or imprisonment.
NOTE.—All Provisions of the Air Commerce Regulations are made a part of the terms hereof as though written herein.

Form 8   (over)

14. U.S. Department of Commerce, Bureau of Air Commerce, aircraft inspection report (a) and license (b), indicating engine power specifications and the fuel capacity of 1,151 gallons. This much-higher-than-reported fuel capacity gave the Electra a fuel endurance time of as much as twenty-eight hours, forty-five minutes. *National Archives, Washington, D.C.*

In reply

SWP 740.0011   --2145

Date: **August 28, 1945**

⌐CDLETTER

This form of communication is used in the interest of speed and economy. If a reply is necessary, address the Department of State, attention of the Division mentioned below.

SPEEDLETTER

To:

    Mr. G. P. Putnam,
    10042 Valley Spring Lane,
    North Hollywood, California.

GPO 16—44742-1

       Following message received for you from Weihsien via American Embassy, Chungking:

         "Camp liberated; all well. Volumes to tell. Love to mother (*)."

        Eldred D. Kuppinger
        Assistant Chief
    Special War Problems Division

(*) Signature omitted.

SWP:VVWaters

         v ᵛ'

DCR - GP-C Unit
nal. ____
Rev. ____ 8-28-45

A true copy of the signed original.

15. Telegram sent to George Palmer Putnam on August 28, 1945, after the liberation of the Weishien, China Civil Assembly Center. *Special War Problems Division, U.S. Department of State*

CHAPTER ELEVEN

Tokyo Rosa

"I'll stake my life that that is not Amelia's voice."
—George Palmer Putnam,
according to Muriel Earhart Morrissey

For what purpose did the Japanese capture and hold Amelia Earhart? Apart from being caught in espionage, what was her value as a long-term prisoner: hostage, pawn, or negotiating or trading chip? Or was there potential propaganda value in holding on to one of America's most acclaimed—and informed—citizens, an establishment wife who was known to be a friend of the president of the United States?

Prior to Japan's surrender, there were rumors that one of the insinuating radio voices known collectively to U.S. servicemen as "Tokyo Rose" belonged to Amelia Earhart.[1] Appearing on programs that originated in Japan and were broadcast throughout the Pacific Theater, these English-speaking women taunted the men with evocative American music and news—all of it bad—about developments in the war and at home. The general tone of the broadcasts was upbeat and lively, but the theme was the futility, hopelessness, and eventual defeat of the Allied war effort. The aim, of course, was to confuse, mislead, and generally demoralize American fighting men.

In response to the rumors about his wife in 1944, George Putnam was given a special commission as a major in the Intelligence Division of the U.S. Army Air Corps and flown to China. Since he could be expected to know Amelia's voice and intonations better than most, his orders were to listen to "Tokyo Rose" broadcasts that were being beamed to troops in the China-Burma-India Theater.[2] Amelia's sister, Muriel, recalls the incident in her book, *Courage Is the Price*:

> After the European D-Day when the collapse of Japanese resistance was imminent, a woman's voice was sometimes heard, broadcasting from Tokyo false information to American forces. Could this "Tokyo Rose" possibly be Amelia, brainwashed to the point of leading her countrymen into enemy traps? Every fiber of GP's being denied the possibility, but he alone in all that vast area could without question identify Amelia's voice, even though weakened and tense from psychological mistreatment.
>
> He made a dangerous three-day trek through Japanese-held territory to reach a Marine Corps radio station near the coast where the broadcast reception was loud and clear. After listening to the voice for less than a minute, GP said decisively, "I'll stake my life that that is not Amelia's voice. It sounds to me as if the woman might have lived in New York, and of course she had been fiendishly well coached, but Amelia—never!"[3]

In fact, Putnam's forceful response raises many more questions than it answers.

"Fiendishly well coached" to what end in 1944? To convince the U.S. that Amelia Earhart was being held as a Japanese prisoner of war? To prove that she had not drowned in the Pacific on July 2, 1937? Who would believe it? What were they trying to achieve?

And why had anyone thought that the voice was Amelia's in the first place? Evidently, our government was not convinced that she was dead. Had this particular "Tokyo Rose" identified herself as Earhart, or had she simply sounded familiar to U.S. military officials listening in China? We may never know, since there are no extant recordings of the woman in question.

The timing seems particularly strange, for the war was virtually over. The Japanese empire lay in ruins, and the Home Islands were cut off, even from one another, by ubiquitous U.S. submarines that sank everything afloat. On a single low-level incendiary raid in July of that year, General Curtis LeMay's 20th Bomber Command rained down a firestorm that devastated most of Tokyo and killed half a million people in one night. Other Japanese cities suffered comparably. In straits so desperate, the use of Amelia Earhart's voice may have been intended only to show that she was alive and still held captive. It goes without saying that the propaganda value of Earhart as a bargaining chip, representative also of the thousands of other U.S. civilians then held captive in Japan and occupied China, would have been immeasurable.

The complete answer undoubtedly lies in two places: in classified U.S. archives, where so many other answers to the Earhart mystery have been found, and in Japanese records. Access to the latter, which have remained closed to researchers, may become possible in the near future, now that wartime Emperor Hirohito has died.

The "Tokyo Rose" speculations have an interesting footnote. During the summer of 1949, an American woman named Iva Ikuko Toguri D'Aquino was put on trial in Federal Court for the Northern District of California, in San Francisco, for eight counts of overt actions against the United States.⁴ Although married to a Portuguese national, she had chosen not to renounce her American citizenship; therefore, her alleged actions constituted treason during wartime, an offense that carried the death penalty. According to the nineteen witnesses who testified, she was the so-called Tokyo Rose.⁵

Other evidence presented during the trial, however, indicated that up to fifteen different women may have been involved in the infamous broadcasts. Moreover, according to materials entered into evidence by D'Aquino's defense attorney, Wayne M. Collins, there may have been no "Tokyo Rose" broadcasts as such at all. The jury and spectators were shocked to learn that a total of forty Allied prisoners of war were used to prepare and perform various programs for the Broadcasting Corporation of Japan. A number of English-speaking female voices were heard on "Humanity Calls," "The Postman Calls," "Light from Asia," "Prisoner's Zero Hour," "Hinomura Hour," and "The Women's Hour." These prisoners were housed in such places as the Dai-Ichi Hotel, the Sanno Hotel, and the Bunka Prison Camp, among other places. Ironically, no female voice on Japanese radio before, during, or after the war ever identified herself as "Tokyo Rose."⁶

Even so, D'Aquino was convicted on one of the eight counts and sentenced to ten years in prison. She would be released from the Women's Federal Penitentiary at Alderson, West Virginia, six years later, with time off for good behavior.

During her trial for treason against the United States, there was testimony about a strange case of treason against Japan in 1944. When Saipan fell to Allied forces on June 15, Radio Tokyo immediately broadcast a news flash about the victory, along with a recording of "The Stars and Stripes Forever." The Kampeitei, the secret police, launched a full-scale investigation, all the more furious because the Sousa march was mistaken for "The Star-Spangled Banner."[7] Presumably, one of the American POWs forced to work at the station was responsible. Was Amelia Earhart numbered among them?

If not, why did Amy Otis Earhart attend the entire Iva Toguri trial? She was a very old woman, in poor health, living still in Medford, Massachusetts, a continent away. Was she hoping, perhaps, to hear some word of her daughter's fate, because she had heard why Putnam was sent to China? Or did she know something definite?

According to the New York Times, Mrs. Earhart had this to say at the conclusion of the trial:

> Amelia told me many things, but there were some things she couldn't tell me. I am convinced she was on some sort of a government mission, probably on verbal orders.[8]

The recollections of Antonio M. Cepada are typical of the remarks made by scores of Saipanese natives interviewed in the 1960s. An employee of the Buick service garage in Agana, Guam, he gave the following account to Major Gervais in 1960, as Police Chief Quintinella listened:

> One summer about two years after I got married, I saw an American girl who was referred to by some as the "American spy woman." She was quartered on the second floor of the Hotel Kobayash Royokan in the summer of 1937. I don't remember any plane crash [other witnesses recalled the crash of a twin-engine plane into Tanapag Harbor at this time], but I saw the girl twice on two separate occasions outside the hotel over a period of two or three months.

I saw her while going to work outside the hotel, which is located in east Garapan village. She wore unusual clothes—a long raincoat belted in the center. The color was faded khaki. She was average height American girl—not short, not extra tall—had thin build. Her hair appeared to be reddish-brown color and cut short like a man's hair, trimmed close in back like a man. She did not wear powder or lipstick as I see other American women wear now.

I did not know how she was caught, but rumor was that she then took secret pictures with flying suit in front hidden camera maybe.[9]

In response to Gervais's questions, Cepada replied that he did not know what had happened to the American woman: "I saw her only twice. Maybe she was deported to Japan. That is all I know."

"Can you describe her facial expression?" Gervais asked. "Or the way she appeared to you?"

"The girl looked soft, very calm. Not expressive. No smile. Seemed to be thinking far away. She didn't notice her surroundings and the people much. Tokyo Rosa was maybe thirty-five years old."

"Why do you call her that?"

"Everyone on Saipan referred to her as Tokyo Rosa. In 1937 Tokyo Rosa meant American spy lady."

"You mean Tokyo Rose on the Japanese radio during the war? That Tokyo Rose?"

Cepada shook his head. "Not that one. Tokyo Rosa in 1937 meant American spy girl. That's all. Nothing else."

Shown a photo of Amelia Earhart, Cepada said, "It looks just like the same woman."

"Did you ever hear of Amelia Earhart?"

"Who?"

"Amelia Earhart. Ever hear of her?"

"Never heard of her."

"Do you know anyone else who might have seen the girl on Saipan?"

"Yes. Carlos Palacious. He was there. And Carlos lives here on Guam now."

Major Gervais, still accompanied by Chief Quintinella, sought out Palacious immediately, so that there was no time for Cepada to contact the man first. In the 1930s, as it turned out, Palacious had been a salesclerk for the Ishi-Shoten, a general-merchandise store located near the Hotel Kobayashi-Royokan in East Garapan. His recollections were fragmentary but vivid:

> I saw the woman only twice in about a three-month period. It was while I was going to and from the store where I worked. The first time, I saw her at a window on the second floor of the hotel. The window was open, and she had on what looked to me like a man's shirt with short sleeves, with an open collar. The girl had short dark reddish-brown hair, cut like man's hair in back, too. . . .
>
> I don't know where she was caught. . . . I never heard anything about a crash . . . only that Tokyo Rosa was an American spy girl and she had taken secret pictures.[10]

"Why," Gervais asked, "do you call her Tokyo Rosa?"

"Tokyo Rosa was my people's expression for American spy girl."

"Could the girl come and go freely from the hotel? Did you see any guards near her?"

"Maybe she could come and go when I didn't see her," Palacious ventured. "I don't think guards were necessary. No one was free to come and go from Saipan without Japanese knowledge and permission. If anyone tried it, they got killed. The Japanese knew everything about everyone."

"How old did the girl look to you?"

"Maybe thirty-four to thirty-six. Hard to tell; I only saw her twice."

"What do you think happened to her?"

"Probably deported to Japan."

Gervais brought out the photograph of Amelia Earhart. Palacious responded, "Face and haircut look like same girl in picture."

"Are you sure?"

"I only know what I saw, and what I have told you is true."

"Have you ever heard of Amelia Earhart?"

"No."

CHAPTER TWELVE

Conclusion?

I hope I've just got to never make it public.
>   —Henry Morgenthau, Jr.,
>   secretary of the treasury and FDR confidant

But what happened next?

According to many Saipanese, Amelia Earhart and Fred Noonan were executed as spies outside the prison at Garapan, but no one interviewed on record has ever been able to state positively that he witnessed the execution of either of the Americans. Over the years, numerous researchers have descended upon the island in search of credible witnesses or evidence, including remains, but the execution theory remains pure speculation.

And from the broad perspective, it does not make much sense. What would the Japanese stand to gain by taking the life of an American who was an international celebrity? More important, what might they lose by killing her? Undoubtedly aware of Earhart's stature and importance, they were far too shrewd to waste a valuable asset that had literally dropped from the sky.

That the officials at the local level might have lacked sophistication is not to the point, for they would not have dared break the political and military "chain of command" back to Tokyo. The more important the decision in any organization, the higher the level at which that decision will be made. Besides, Earhart's proud captors, eager to take credit for bagging such a prize, would definitely have notified the imperial-Japanese government.

At the highest levels, the conventional response would have been to try to get maximum advantage from Earhart's aviation expertise, her well-known closeness to FDR and his administration, and her propaganda value, even if she was to be executed in the end. From that point of view, it is logical that she would have been taken to Tokyo, just as it is logical for her to be taken from the Marshall Islands to the highest political and military center in the immediate region, Saipan.

And this conclusion is not mere speculation. An American Jesuit priest detained in the capital as a prisoner of war happened to overhear two Japanese military officers discussing the truth about Earhart in "guarded phrases" late in July 1937. According to Father Francis Briggs, who was fluent in Japanese, they knew for certain that an American woman pilot caught spying over their fortified zones was being held on Saipan but would soon be brought to Tokyo.[1]

When Father Briggs was repatriated in 1946, he contacted the FBI in order to make a report of this startling conversation, but he was given the distinct impression that the agency was uninterested in his information. Today two boxes of material concerning the priest are on file in the National Archives and Records Administration, Diplomatic Branch. They remain classified.

Why did the U.S. government not act upon such evidence and formally, officially investigate Japan's involvement in Earhart's disappearance? Why maintain the fiction, in effect, that Tokyo was not in any way involved?

Perhaps the explanation for FDR's inaction lies in the denouement of a similar situation that would occur in 1960. An American pilot flying a high-altitude secret photo-reconnaissance mission was discovered in action, shot down, and captured thirteen hundred miles inside Soviet territory. Would the Eisenhower administration have launched a public investigation of the fate of Francis Gary Powers if the Russians had kept quiet about the incident? Would the Russians have said anything publicly if they had not sensed the opportunity for propaganda advantage in the Cold War? Without that motive, the Russians might have said nothing, the U.S. would not have been able to make any kind of public protest, and the world would never have heard of Powers.

Specifically ordered to obtain "a quantitative analysis of Japanese ship strength and military construction in the Marshall Islands,"[2] Earhart was definitely the Gary Powers of 1937, and FDR would have just as much reason as Eisenhower to disavow U.S. involvement in her espionage flight. As for Amelia herself, even though she was a civilian, she would have been subject to the ancient, unwritten cardinal rule of espionage: If you are captured, you are on your own—we never knew you. In anticipation of that eventuality, she would almost certainly have been advised to plead ignorance, ineptitude, navigational error, or the like.

For their part, the Japanese would not have wanted to bring world attention to bear upon the object of that flight, their vast construction of ships, deep harbors, airfields, and military installations throughout the Mandates. Tangible evidence of these illegal activities would

have enabled the U.S. or one of the signatories of the
Versailles Treaty to go to the World Court and demand
an immediate order granting authority to conduct inspec-
tions of the area. The implications for Japan's national
ambitions would have been staggering.

But why did the U.S. government keep silent after the
war? How much more did they learn after the defeat of
Japan? Why are so many aspects of the Earhart affair still
hidden in confidential files?

When American forces invaded Saipan in 1944, they
confiscated tons of documents and photographs found in
the enemy's Pacific Island Headquarters, including the
pouch found by marine gunner Wallack. They also gathered up records and materials that had belonged to the
native population, along with records of the so-called
South Seas Development Corporation. In addition, the
441st U.S. Army Counterintelligence Corps also conducted interrogations of the Japanese secret policemen
based there about the events preceding the war. The results were also shipped to the U.S., with the most sensitive intelligence information screened by the Joint Intelligence Bureau in Honolulu.[3]

But the record of the Roosevelt administration's
knowledge of the true story goes back even further.

On May 13, 1938, the White House called Secretary of
the Treasury Henry Morgenthau, Jr., interrupting him in
a meeting with a special request. Eleanor Roosevelt
wanted to have a copy of all of the information he had on
Amelia Earhart's disappearance the year before. The first
lady was not someone easily put off by a Cabinet officer,
but Morgenthau demurred. That information, he explained, must never be made public. He did, however,

explicitly state that at least some of the information, the real story about the final hours and minutes of the flight, was contained in the *Itasca*'s logs (which have been released only piecemeal over the past fifty years).

According to Mrs. Roosevelt's secretary, Malvina "Tommy" Scheider, he also said, "I hope I've just got to never make it public," adding that it would completely ruin the reputation of Amelia Earhart. (See source notes for a complete transcript of the conversation.)[4]

The secretary of the navy, too, had an Earhart file, which was eventually placed under Top Secret classification in the office of the flag secretary to the chief of naval operations, located in Room 2052 of the old Navy Department building on Constitution Avenue.[5]

Carroll F. Harris, now a retired California highway patrolman living in the Sacramento area, served as a navy photographer assigned to work under Flag Secretary Admiral J. R. Smedberg. He was given a high-level security clearance so that he could photograph secret records on 16mm microfilm, including documents in both the Naval Operations general files (OP-20G) and the Office of Naval Intelligence (OP-16-ONI). He has recalled that the Earhart files occupied three-quarters of a file-cabinet drawer, including the following:

1. *The navy's reasons for its clandestine participation in the Amelia Earhart world flight and speculation about the possible impact (including political fallout) of disclosure of any details of the mission.* In particular, the navy wanted to hide the U.S. attempt to photograph Truk Atoll and other areas in the Mandates in order to obtain a quantitative analysis of Japanese shipping in the area.[6]

2. *Details of the precautions taken to keep secret Earhart's actual route from Lae to Howland Island.* The records show that she

was able to take a different, longer flight path than her publicly announced itinerary because the navy had installed the
military-specification Wasp Senior engines in her plane.[7]

3. *Specifications calling for an increased wingspan along with
structural enhancements to a specifically equipped, structurally
modified Lockheed Electra that was substituted for the Model 10E
Earhart crashed in Hawaii.*[8]

4. *Complete details, including photographs, of the installation
and operation of two Fairchild aerial-survey cameras in the lower
fuselage bay of the aircraft, along with a modification of the
plane's electrical system to accommodate the additional electrical
loads imposed on the generators by this other equipment.*[9]

5. *The addition of more powerful Bendix communications radios,
capable of transmitting over much longer distances than anything
commercially available at the time.* In addition, special high-
frequency direction-finding equipment was installed, as were
extra, more powerful batteries. According to the documenta-
tion, one aim of the mission was to test this new ADF during
the overflight of Truk for efficacy in pinpoint long-range aerial navigation.[10]

6. *Details of the arrangements for personnel of the Office of Naval
Intelligence (ONI) to recover the film and equipment secretly and
swiftly upon completion of the mission.* Clearly, the navy considered it imperative to retain total control over this material at
all times and keep it completely secret.[11]

7. *Plans for part of the preparatory work on the Electra to be
executed in Miami, including calibration of equipment.* It is clear
that final testing was scheduled for the latter part of the flight
but prior to departure from Lae.[12]

8. *Details concerning storage of the aircraft at the Alameda
Naval Air Station, along with an outline of the work to be performed there.* (The records indicate that modifications took
place not only at Alameda but also at March Field and Lockheed's Burbank facility.)[13]

Another file on the Earhart mission may have been maintained in FDR's so-called Map Room, where the most closely guarded secrets of his presidency were kept. This most restricted area of FDR's White House was memorably described by Eric Larrabee in his book, *Commander in Chief*:

> Roosevelt's Map Room was peculiarly his own, a characteristic expression of his working habits. The door said, "No admittance," and indeed no one was allowed inside but the President, Harry Hopkins, the Joint Chiefs, Captain McCrea [Roosevelt's personal aide] presidential secretary Grace Tully . . . and the around-the-clock Army and Navy duty officers.
>
> Here, too, was what the President called "the Magic Book," containing the latest reports from Magic, the cryptanalysts who had broken enemy codes. Here also were kept action reports, future plans, records of decisions, and the President's communications with other wartime leaders, making this the most extensive collection of secret documents in Washington.
>
> Information is control, as Roosevelt well knew. . . . He cannily [sent] outgoing messages through the Army and received incoming messages through the Navy, so that only his own set of files in the Map Room was complete.[14]

Roosevelt's reliance upon the Map Room as a repository for his most sensitive files is significant here, because it is highly possible that part or all of twelve boxes of files on Amelia Earhart that turned up after the war were kept there while he was still alive. That in itself would prove their fundamental importance to the nation's defense efforts.

If not kept there, however, they were in the care of Secretary Morgenthau. What is known is that the files include information about Earhart's fate, as well as specific details of discussions of the matter in a Cabinet meeting July 24, 1937 (six days after the navy's search was called off). The participants, informed that the two Americans had been captured by the Japanese, discussed what, if anything, could be done. (Morgenthau, under whose direct jurisdiction the bulk of the government's involvement had been conducted, was en route to Honolulu and could not attend.) This information about the nature of the files, at this writing stored in Sub-Basement 33A of the Main Treasury Building on Pennsylvania Avenue, was provided by a Treasury Department employee in mid-1988. It seems probable that the materials Morgenthau mentioned to his secretary are included as well.

To date, the Treasury Department has not granted a FOIA request for access to the twelve boxes of "Morgenthau files" or agreed to characterize their contents.

Perhaps other materials also made their way into the boxes in the basement of the Treasury Department.

On August 16, 1945, Amelia's best friend, Jackie Cochran, then commandant of the Woman's Auxiliary Service Pilots (WASPs), was sent from the Philippines to Tokyo by General H. H. "Hap" Arnold, ostensibly for the purpose of "investigating the role of Japanese women in aviation during the [air] war effort. . . ."[15] At this point, no official U.S. military or Allied Forces contingent had yet arrived to secure the capital. General MacArthur and Fleet Admiral Chester Nimitz, with their combined forces, were more than twenty days away.

When Cochran was escorted through the Imperial Air Force headquarters inside the Dai Ichi Palace, she found "there were . . . several files on Amelia Earhart. . . ." Soon afterward, General George Kenney, commander-in-chief of the U.S. Far East Air Forces, ordered an aircraft put at her disposal so that she could fly into China, even though travel there was restricted at the time to the highest-ranking military officers.[16] (General Albert C. Wedemeyer, the commanding general of the region, had closed the Chinese Theater for two principal reasons, the lack of food and provisions, combined with the inability of the U.S. military to provide adequate security.)

Meanwhile, Francis Cardinal Spellman, military vicar general of the U.S. forces, arrived in Tokyo to join Cochran. Late on August 20, they took off for Chungking, joined by five unidentified Roman Catholic nuns who had been held in Japan as prisoners of war and were being evacuated. During her brief stopover in the Chinese city, Cochran met with General George E. Stratemeyer, commander of the U.S. occupational forces in the Chinese Theater, and later with Madame Chiang Kai-shek at Kuomintang headquarters.

In *The Stars at Noon*, Cochran wrote that she had asked her friend "Strat" to let her send a cable directly to Secretary of War Robert Patterson in Washington. According to her account, she wanted to ask Patterson to rescind an order canceling the special status of war correspondents in China, because she felt that the decision did not allow the writers enough time to complete their work and leave the country under the protection of U.S. forces and protocol. Unfortunately, the original order had been issued by General Wedemeyer and sustained by Stratemeyer. In a discussion Cochran described as "heated," the latter informed her that, because of the subject matter, she "would be disappointed to learn that that cable would not go through because it would be stopped by the censorship."[17]

Cochran countered that, if the U.S. military would not cooperate, her cable "would go out, if necessary, in the diplomatic pouch of the Canadian Ambassador, and be sent to Washington from Canada."[18] As it happened, this particular diplomat was General Victor Odlum, her husband's cousin. A determined Stratemeyer barked that he "could probably even stop that."[19]

This lively story, of course, makes no sense. Jackie Cochran was traveling on military orders. Her rather unvarnished personal style notwithstanding, she could not have assumed such a belligerent attitude toward a U.S. Army commanding general in charge of occupied territory. An appeal to the secretary of war to countermand a theater commander's order could have provoked a serious charge of insubordination. In fact, the evidence suggests that the truth was very different from the account in *The Stars at Noon*.

First, what was the real reason Jackie Cochran had flown to Chungking? The minor problem with the journalists was not sufficient motive for her flight, or for her altercation with "Strat." Second, why did she have to communicate directly with Secretary Patterson? It would have been standard practice to work through the man who cut her orders, General Arnold. Third, there is no record in U.S. military and Department of State diplomatic-post files of the telegram Cochran claimed she eventually did send through the Canadian embassy in late August 1945.

We will probably never be able to ascertain the truth about Cochran's peculiar trip, but we can briskly dismiss her cover story. Assessment of the possible role of Japanese women in military aviation was not so critical a U.S. objective that a prominent citizen would have to be sent into Japan so soon after cease-fire that her safety was in doubt. Besides, the answer was as readily available in any good library as in the smoldering ruins of war-torn Japan and China: because of the well-known norms of Japanese culture, women played virtually no role at all in the air war.

For what reason, then, would Cochran risk her life to get to the Dai Ichi files as quickly as possible? And risk a very nasty incident, if not court-martial, to get a message back to Washington?

The answer might lie in a telegram that actually *was* sent from the Canadian embassy to the War Department late that August, the only priority telegram sent from Wei-shien, China:

CAMP LIBERATED ALL WELL VOLUMES TO TELL LOVE TO MOTHER

This telegram, released by the U.S. government during the week of July 2, 1987, as newspapers around the world ran stories keyed to the fiftieth anniversary of the disappearance of Amelia Earhart and Fred Noonan, was dispatched from the Canadian government in Montreal for domestic delivery by U.S. radiogram. The addressee was George Palmer Putnam, 10042 Valley Spring Lane, North Hollywood, California.

The State Department entity that declassified the contents was identified as the "Special War Problems Branch." The file was labeled "Earhart, Amelia." It bore the file number PW/8-2145; "PW" was a designation used only for prisoners of war.

Did Amelia's old friend discover where she was held and race to get the information to the highest levels of the U.S. government?

To this question, as to so many that surround the mystery of Amelia Earhart's disappearance, there is no single definitive solution provided by a "smoking gun." So far as can be determined or sensibly inferred from the evidence available, there is no secret "Amelia Earhart file" stashed away somewhere in the vaults of the U.S. government with the complete details of what happened to her on July 2, 1937.

In the research and writing of this book, however, a body of circumstantial evidence has been gathered that is both comprehensive and convincing, particularly since there is absolutely no evidence extant to prove that Earhart perished in the Pacific Ocean. This kind of reasoning is called, in law, the theory of a preponderance of evidence. It is used as the basis for deciding cases for which no single definitive solution or *corpus delicti* exists.

And, in fact, the evidence we do have fits together quite well under that theory. The documentary evidence that has been discovered does clearly indicate government involvement, despite the long-standing denials from so many official quarters. The testimony of individuals is in agreement on the key points that suggest a credible solution of the mystery.

We can confidently sketch out the main outline. Long before her first equatorial attempt, in mid- to late 1936, Amelia Earhart began a correspondence with the Roosevelt administration that resulted in a liaison for the planning of the flight. This initial liaison evolved into close cooperation with the navy, along with the Commerce, Interior, and Treasury departments, in the scheme to establish a landing facility on Howland Island. Later still, the idea that she would be an invaluable aerial spy somehow crystallized in top U.S. military and government circles; she became key to a plot to obtain intelligence information about Japan's illegal activities in the Marshall and Caroline islands of the South Pacific.

To that end, as the government's own documents prove in detail, Earhart was given a specially built Electra 12 while the public was deliberately led to believe that she was flying her repaired Electra 10E. In other words, the watching world thought her plane had much less range, speed, and altitude capability than it actually did have.

In much the same vein, almost everyone responsible for guiding or monitoring the progress of the flight was kept in the dark. Whether civilian or military, most of them did not know the true purpose of the mission. In the final stages of the operation, they were either excluded from participation or flatly deceived about Earhart's intentions and actual whereabouts at crucial points.

More than half a century later, it is perhaps clearer that there are many gaps in the supposed record of the flight. For what happened in the crucial month from June 1 through July 2, for example, we must rely exclusively on Earhart's notes; there is no other firsthand account. Yet she does not report at all on her activities during significant periods of time in late June.

Nor can we rely upon the government reports that have for so long been taken at face value and used as the basis for the traditional versions of the mystery; they have been proved false at several pivotal points. As we have seen, correspondence exchanged during preparations for the flight belie the fabrication that it was a purely civilian undertaking. In addition, the navy's help in preparing the Electra, the gaps in the *Itasca* logs, Morgenthau's determination to suppress the truth—all confirm that there was, and continues to be, a government cover-up of the facts.

And the failure of the navy's massive search only serves to reinforce that conclusion: the shadow agenda of searching the islands for Japanese fortifications meant that the special task force did not concentrate on the Line group until it was too late to find and rescue Earhart and Noonan. As so many witnesses have convincingly testified, the flyers were taken aboard a Japanese ship sometime during the period July 5–7. Subsequently, Noonan was given medical attention aboard the vessel at Jaluit Island, and the Electra was off-loaded at Taroa Island. Meanwhile, the

U.S. government was fully aware of what occurred from July 2 through 7, as is clear from the comments of Eugene Vidal, who informed the president, and Secretary Morgenthau, who undoubtedly discussed the matter with FDR as well.

Earhart and Noonan were taken to Saipan; certainly Amelia was seen by scores of witnesses and photographed by at least one. Later, according to several very suggestive indications, they apparently survived for an indefinite time as prisoners of war. It is probable that Amelia was held in Japan and China throughout the conflict; in fact, at least one eyewitness reports seeing her in a prison camp in Weishien. One tantalizingly persistent account has Amelia supposedly returning to the U.S. and assuming a new identity.

But there is much more to be told, and more documents to tell it—if they can be found and declassified. The materials used for this book took many years to locate, and, as I discussed in the introduction, further persistence and patience in the face of bureaucratic obstacles to their release. In addition to the documents obtained and reproduced here, several others of potential importance are still being held by a resistant government. It may be many more years, therefore, before all of the relevant classified records can be examined.

Even so, as the revelations discussed in this book should show clearly, the story of what happened to Amelia Earhart and Fred Noonan is at last falling into place, piece by piece. Each new discovery underscores a fundamental, and disturbing, fact: the truth conflicts with the official and traditionally accepted versions. That will continue to be the case, without doubt, as more information is gradually released by the Treasury Department, the National Archives, the FBI, and the Naval Security Group Command.

Despite the unsettling behavior of officialdom, how-ever, we must not lose sight of the great courage and patri-otism Amelia Earhart displayed in her last flight: govern-ment secrecy, in fact, has deprived her of her fair measure of glory as an authentic American hero. A pacifist who may have undergone a profound spiritual struggle before deciding to become involved in a military mission, she pursued two goals in her espionage: the protection of U.S. national security, and the prevention of war in the Pacific.

In a very real sense, whatever the details of her fate, she gave her life for her country, as did her navigator, Fred Noonan. She would not have regretted taking the risk.

History must be accurate and complete; in a free society, no effort should be spared to see that it is so.

For the opportunity to do this and to be involved in one of the most intriguing adventures of all time, I shall be always grateful to you, Amelia, wherever you are.

—Randall Brink

Notes

CHAPTER 1: Lae

1. *New York Herald-Tribune*, July 2, 1937, p. 1.
2. Amelia Earhart, *Last Flight* (New York: Harcourt, Brace, 1937), p. 196.
3. Fred Goerner, *The Search for Amelia Earhart* (New York: Doubleday, 1966), p. 16.
4. Earhart, *Last Flight*, p. 45.
5. Ibid.
6. Ibid.
7. Ibid., p. 164.
8. Author interviews with Carroll F. Harris, December 1983. Harris referred to files maintained in the office of the Chief of Naval Operations, and of Flag Secretary J. R. Smedburg, as well as the files of the secretary of the navy, Naval Intelligence Section Op-20-G, and Op-16-ONI maintained by the Office of the Judge Advocate General in Room 2052 of the Navy Department building, Washington, D.C.
9. Mary S. Lovell, *The Sound of Wings: The Life of Amelia Earhart* (New York: St. Martin's, 1989), p. 245.
10. Joe Klass, *Amelia Earhart Lives* (New York: McGraw-Hill, 1970), p. 158. Fred Noonan, whose only military experience prior to his disappearance in 1937 was with the British merchant-marine service in World War I, held a U.S. Navy Reserve commission as lieutenant commander.

11. Klass, *Amelia Earhart Lives*, p. 9, quoting an interview with James Collopy by Major Joseph Gervais, USAF.
12. Goerner, *Search for Amelia Earhart*, p. 272.
13. Emile Gauvreau, *The Wild Blue Yonder* (New York: E. P. Dutton, 1944), p. 174. In a chapter titled "Prelude to Pearl Harbor," Gauvreau quotes Secretary of the Navy Claude A. Swanson:

> It was incredible under the circumstances to believe the Earhart plane could have disappeared without a trace unless every matchstick of it had been deliberately destroyed. This is a powder keg. Any public discussion of it will furnish the torch for the explosion.

CHAPTER 2: the Heroine

1. Mary S. Lovell, *The Sound of Wings: The Life of Amelia Earhart* (New York: St. Martin's, 1989), p. 13.
2. Ibid.
3. Ibid.
4. Jean L. Backus, *Letters from Amelia: An Intimate Portrait of Amelia Earhart* (New York: Beacon Press, 1982), p. 18.
5. Ibid.
6. Ibid.
7. Lovell, *Sound of Wings*, p. 21.
8. Ibid. p. 16.
9. Letter from Amelia Earhart to Virginia Parks, March 6, 1914, from Backus, *Letters from Amelia*, p. 21.
10. Ibid., p. 22.
11. Amelia Earhart, *The Fun of It* (New York: Brewer, Warren and Putnam, 1932), p. 19.
12. Amelia Earhart, *Last Flight* (New York: Harcourt, Brace, 1937), p. 5.
13. Backus, *Letters from Amelia*, p. 47.
14. Lovell, *Sound of Wings*, p. 27.
15. Ibid., p. 29.
16. Earhart, *The Fun of It*, p. 23.
17. Lovell, *Sound of Wings*, p. 30.
18. Ibid., p. 32.
19. Earhart, *The Fun of It*, p. 24.
20. Ibid.
21. Ibid.

22. Lovell, *Sound of Wings*, p. 33.
23. Ibid.
24. Neta Snook Southern, *I Taught Amelia Earhart to Fly* (New York: Vantage, 1974), p. 1.

CHAPTER 3: Fame

1. From recorded remarks made by Fred Goerner at the National Air and Space Museum, Smithsonian Institution, Washington, D.C., June 18, 1982.
2. Neta Snook Southern, *I Taught Amelia Earhart to Fly* (New York: Vantage, 1974), pp. 102–5.
3. Amelia Earhart, *20 Hrs. 40 Min.* (New York: G. P. Putnam's Sons, 1929), pp. 75–76.
4. Ibid., p. 67.
5. Ibid., p. 65.
6. Mary S. Lovell, *The Sound of Wings: The Life of Amelia Earhart* (New York: St. Martin's, 1989), p. 39.
7. Fred Goerner, *The Search for Amelia Earhart* (New York: Doubleday, 1966), p. 17.
8. Ibid., p. 14.
9. Lovell, *Sound of Wings*, p. 45.
10. Ibid., p. 46.
11. Amelia Earhart, *Last Flight* (New York: Harcourt, Brace, 1937), p. 7.
12. Ibid., p. 8.
13. Ibid.
14. Lovell, *Sound of Wings*, p. 115.
15. Ibid., p. 112.
16. Ibid.
17. Ibid., p. 113.
18. Ibid., p. 115.
19. Earhart, *20 Hrs. 40 Min.*, p. 170.
20. Earhart, *Last Flight*, p. 10.
21. Ibid., p. 13.
22. Elinor Smith, *Aviatrix*, (New York: Harcourt Brace Jovanovich, 1981), p. 238.
23. Lovell, *Sound of Wings*, p. 165.
24. Letter from Amelia Earhart to George Palmer Putnam, February 7, 1931 (the day of their wedding).
25. Lovell, *Sound of Wings*, p. 169.
26. Ibid.

27. *New York Times*, June 20, 1931.
28. Earhart, *Last Flight*, p. 15.
29. Ibid.
30. Goerner, *Search for Amelia Earhart*, p. 25.
31. Ibid.
32. Author interviews with Walter B. McMenamy, Los Angeles, California, June–August 1980.
33. Ibid.
34. Earhart, *Last Flight*, p. 23.
35. Ibid., p. 24.
36. Jean L. Backus, *Letters from Amelia: An Intimate Portrait of Amelia Earhart* (New York: Beacon Press, 1982) p. 98.

CHAPTER 4: Spy?

1. Letter from Amelia Earhart to Walter McMenamy, March 4, 1937. Author files.
2. *Los Angeles Times*, Wednesday, March 10, 1937, p. B-1.
3. National Archives Record Group 80, U.S. Navy Classified Files, file A-4-5(5), box 146, Microfilm Records.
4. Memorandum of Admiral William D. Leahy, U.S. Navy chief of staff, to President Roosevelt, National Archives Record Group 80.
5. Memorandum of President Roosevelt to Secretary of State Cordell Hull, February 19, 1936. (Reproduced herein, illus. 1a) Presidential Private File, Franklin D. Roosevelt Library, Hyde Park, N.Y.
6. Brief of Rex Martin, director of air commerce, U.S. Department of Commerce, for the president, April 8, 1935. Ibid.
7. Memorandum of Secretary of State Cordell Hull to the president, February 18, 1936. (See illus. 1b)
8. FDR to Hull, February 19, 1936.
9. Amelia Earhart, *Last Flight* (New York: Harcourt, Brace, 1937), p. 51.
10. Ibid.
11. Quoted by Fred Goerner, recorded remarks, National Air and Space Museum, Smithsonian Institution, Washington, D.C., June 18, 1982.
12. Lockheed Aircraft Corporation bill of sale. Also, the customer name "Livingston" appeared on Lockheed Aircraft Corporation interdepartmental memorandum dated March 21, 1936.
13. Earhart, *Last Flight*, p. 43.

14. Ibid., p. 52.

15. Eric Larrabee, *Commander in Chief: Franklin D. Roosevelt and His Commanders* (New York: Harper & Row, 1987), p. 214.

16. Quoted by Goerner, NASM.

17. George Palmer Putnam, *Soaring Wings* (New York: Harcourt, Brace, 1939), p. 261.

18. Earhart, *Last Flight*, p. 63.

19. Ibid., pp. 68–69.

20. Author interviews with Walter B. McMenamy and Karl E. Pierson, Los Angeles, California June–August 1980. Prior to Amelia Earhart's accident at Luke Field, Hawaii, the radio technicians, organized at her request by Walter McMenamy, worked closely with Amelia as she made the world-flight preparations. They were to convey all radio transmissions received from the Earhart flight directly to the *Los Angeles Times,* for their exclusive use in publishing a chronicle of the flight. For the second flight attempt, however, this plan was scrapped.

21. Earhart, *Last Flight*, p. 69.

22. Interviews with McMenamy, June–August 1980.

23. Earhart, *Last Flight*, p. 68.

24. According to Margo de Carrie, aide and secretary to Amelia Earhart, and keeper of the Putnams' Hollywood, California, home, prior to the Luke Field incident, she was responsible for bookkeeping and paying bills arising from Amelia's flying activities. After that, however, no bills were received or paid, and she was given the impression that such expenses were being paid thenceforth by the U.S. government. She stated that, during April–June 1937, William T. Miller of the U.S. Department of Commerce Bureau of Airports was installed at the Hollywood house, and took over all details of the flight-planning operation that were conducted there. (It may also be worth noting here that Miller was with George Putnam in Oakland when the telephone call came informing them of the Luke Field crash.)

CHAPTER 5: War

1. G. S. Allen, *A Short Economic History of Japan* (London, 1981), p. 141.

2. Paul Kennedy, *The Rise and Fall of the Great Powers* (New York: Random House, 1987), pp. 301–2.

3. Emile Gauvreau, *The Wild Blue Yonder* (New York: E. P. Dutton, 1944), p. 174.

4. Ibid.

5. Bender Altschul, *The Chosen Instrument*

6. U.S. Naval Intelligence (ONI) reports of Korean merchant-marine agents, U.S. Navy Classified Files, Modern Military Branch, National Archives and Records Service, Washington, D.C.

CHAPTER 6: Reverse Course

1. Amelia Earhart, *Last Flight* (New York: Harcourt, Brace, 1937), p. 45.

2. Author interviews with Margo de Carrie, Los Angeles, California, August 1980.

3. Memorandum from Rex L. Martin, director of air commerce for the Department of Commerce, to President Roosevelt, April 8, 1935; memorandum from Secretary of State Cordell Hull to President Roosevelt, February 18, 1936; memorandum from FDR to Hull, February 19, 1936, Presidential Papers, FDR Library, Hyde Park, New York.

4. Memorandum from Martin to President Roosevelt, April 8, 1935.

5. Gordon Prange, *At Dawn We Slept* (New York: Penguin, 1981), p. 574.

6. Earhart, *Last Flight*, p. 68.

7. Interviews with de Carrie, August 1980.

8. Ibid.

9. Earhart, *Last Flight*, p. 67.

10. Ibid.

11. Author interviews with Walter McMenamy, Los Angeles, California, June–August 1980.

12. Letter from AE to W. B. McMenamy, March 4, 1937.

13. Interviews with McMenamy, June–August 1980.

14. Author interviews with R. T. Elliot, Katherine Station, Arizona, May 20, 1982.

15. Earhart, *Last Flight*, p. 70.

16. Fred Goerner, *The Search for Amelia Earhart* (New York: Doubleday, 1966), p. 32.

17. Ibid.

18. Interviews with McMenamy, June–August 1980.

19. Ibid.

20. Letter from Lloyd Roger to Joe Gervais, June 30, 1977.

CHAPTER 7: The Attempt

1. Author interviews with Walter McMenamy, Los Angeles, California, June–August 1980.
2. Amelia Earhart, *Last Flight* (New York: Harcourt, Brace, 1937), p. 84.
3. Ibid., p. 91.
4. Ibid., p. 94.
5. Ibid., p. 62.
6. Ibid., p. 97.
7. Ibid., p. 113.
8. Ibid., p. 126.
9. Ibid., p. 128.
10. Ibid., p. 129.
11. Ibid., p. 131.
12. Ibid., p. 132.
13. Letter from Fred Noonan to Mary Beatrice Noonan, July 11, 1937.
14. Earhart, *Last Flight*, p. 171.
15. Ibid., p. 171.
16. Ibid., p. 168
17. Ibid., p. 182.
18. Ibid., p. 189.

CHAPTER 8: Lost

1. Cruise Log of the USCG cutter *Itasca*, July 2–18, 1937, U.S. Navy Narrative Reports of Search for Amelia Earhart, Record Group 80, General Files of the U.S. Navy.
2. Ibid.
3. Ibid.
4. Ibid.
5. Ibid.
6. Ibid.
7. Ibid.

CHAPTER 9: SOS

1. Report of Nauru Island radio operator, incorporated into the U.S. Navy Search Group report. Microfilm Records, National Archives and Records Service, Washington, D.C.
2. Pan American Airways radio operator report, included in U.S.

Navy Narrative Reports of Search for Amelia Earhart, Record Group 80, General Files of the U.S. Navy.

3. Ibid. These signals were also received in Los Angeles by Walter B. McMenamy, Karl E. Pierson, and Guy Dennis.

4. Author interviews with Walter McMenamy, Los Angeles, California, June–August 1980.

5. *Itasca* radio reports, in U.S. Navy Reports of Search for Earhart.

6. Dispatches between Secretary of State Cordell Hull, Japanese Ambassador Joseph C. Grew, and Imperial Japanese Naval Ministry, July 2–18, 1937, State Department files.

7. Ibid.

8. Ibid.

9. Ibid.

10. The disclosure that the *Itasca* intercepted and obtained a "fix" or relative bearing (direction) and distance of these radio signals is revealing, for several reasons:

    1. It indicated that the *Itasca* had the capability of receiving the signals and interpreting the direction and distance of their source, something they were incapable of doing three days earlier, when the plane was still in the air.

    2. The dispatch confirms and corroborates reports of the receipt of the signals by Pan American Airways operator(s) at Wake Island, the U.S. Navy at Honolulu, and the operators in Los Angeles.

    3. The words "still afloat" indicate that the navy and Coast Guard were still proceeding on the assumption that, in that direction relative to Howland Island, and at that approximate distance (281 miles), there was no landmass. It also reflects assumptions about aircraft speed and fuel duration that were inaccurate.

    4. The message confirms that the Electra alighted on land, northwest of Howland, such that the radio equipment aboard was still capable of transmitting.

    5. Ray Rosenbaum *Witness to the Execution: The Odyssey of Amelia Earhart* (Frederick, Colo.: Renaissance House, 1988), p. 17.

    6. Interviews with McMenamy, June–August 1980.

CHAPTER 10: Found

1. Author interview with Bilimon Amaron, Majuro, Marshall Islands, June 1984.

2. Ibid.

3. Interview by Joseph Gervais with John and Dwight Heine, Majuro, Marshall Islands, May 1982.

4. Ibid.

5. U.S. Military Reconnaissance photo, illus. 11.

6. Joe Klass, *Amelia Earhart Lives* (New York: McGraw-Hill, 1970).

7. Fred Goerner, *The Search for Amelia Earhart* (New York: Doubleday, 1966).

8. Excerpted from interviews by Major Joseph Gervais, USAF, Guam, 1960, portions of which also appeared in Klass, *Amelia Earhart Lives*, pp. 67–93.

9. Ibid.

10. See photo, illus. 10.

11. Diaries of Henry Morgenthau, Presidential Papers, FDR Library, Hyde Park, New York.

12. Author interview with Katherine (Vidal) Smith, 1983.

CHAPTER 11: Tokyo Rosa

1. Muriel Earhart Morrissey, *Courage Is the Price* (Wichita, Kan.: McCormick-Armstrong, 1963), p. 14.

2. Ibid.

3. Ibid.

4. Trial proceedings, *United States* v. *Toguri*, Federal Court for the Northern District of California, July 12, 1949.

5. Masayo Duus, *Tokyo Rose: Orphan of the Pacific* (Tokyo: Kodansha International, 1979), p. 12.

6. Ibid., p. 14.

7. Ibid.

8. *New York Times*, October 6, 1949.

9. Interviews by Major Joseph Gervais with Antonio Cepada, Guam, 1960.

10. Interview by Major Joseph Gervais with Carlos Palacious, Guam, 1960.

CHAPTER 12: Conclusion?

1. Report of Fr. Francis Briggs, S.J., to U.S. Department of Justice, Federal Bureau of Investigation, upon repatriation aboard hospital ship SS *Gripsholm*, Special War Problems Branch, U.S. Department of State Classified Files, Diplomatic Branch, National Archives and Records Service, Washington, D.C.

2. Files of Office of Chief of Naval Operations, referred to in author interviews with Carroll F. Harris interviews, December 1983.

3. Records of the 441st U.S. Army Counterintelligence Corps in regard to occupation of Saipan, Mariana Islands, 1944.

4. Telephone transcript of conversation between Henry Morgenthau, Jr., and Malvina Scheider, secretary to Eleanor Roosevelt, May 13, 1938, 9:30 A.M. (reproduced herein, illus. 12), Presidential Papers FDR Library, Hyde Park, New York.

5. Interviews with C. Harris, December 1983.

6. Ibid.

7. Ibid.

8. Ibid.

9. Ibid.

10. Ibid.

11. Ibid.

12. Ibid.

13. Ibid.

14. Eric Larrabee, *Commander in Chief: Franklin D. Roosevelt and His Commanders* (New York: Harper & Row, 1987), pp. 22–23.

15. Jacqueline Cochran, *The Stars at Noon* (New York: Atlantic-Little, Brown, 1954), p. 166.

16. Ibid.

17. Ibid.

18. Ibid., p. 167.

19. Ibid.

Index